100 Plants *to*
FEED THE BIRDS

Turn Your Home Garden into
a Healthy Bird Habitat

LAURA ERICKSON

Storey Publishing

The mission of Storey Publishing is to serve our customers by
publishing practical information that encourages
personal independence in harmony with the environment.

Edited by Deborah Burns
Art direction and book design by Erin Dawson
Text production by Liseann Karandisecky
Indexed by Samantha Miller

Cover photography by © CatLane/iStock.com, front, r. 2 c.l.; © David Pool Photo/stock.adobe.com, front, r. 1 c.;
© eqroy/stock.adobe.com, front, r. 2 r.; © frank mcclintock/EyeEm/stock.adobe.com, front, r. 1 r.; © Holcy/iStock
.com, back, b.r.; © inho Lee/iStock.com, spine; Joshua J. Cotten/Unsplash, front, t.; © Laura Erickson, back, t. &
b.l.; © Maria Brzostowska/stock.adobe.com, front, r. 1 l.; © Mary Lynn Strand/stock.adobe.com, front, r. 2 c.r.;
© Mircea Costina/stock.adobe.com, back, b.c.; © nd700/stock.adobe.com, front, r. 2 l.; © Nina/stock.adobe.com,
front, r. 1 c.l.; © seven75/iStock.com, front, r. 2 c.; © TOMO/stock.adobe.com, front, r. 1 c.r.
Interior photography credits appear on page 255
Maps and icons by Ilona Sherratt © Storey Publishing, LLC

Text © 2022 by Laura Erickson

Storey books are available at special discounts when purchased in bulk for premiums and sales promotions as
well as for fund-raising or educational use. Special editions or book excerpts can also be created to specification.
For details, please call 800-827-8673, or send an email to sales@storey.com.

Storey Publishing
210 MASS MoCA Way
North Adams, MA 01247
storey.com

Printed in China through World Print
10 9 8 7 6 5 4 3 2 1

Library of Congress Cataloging-in-Publication Data on file

This book is dedicated to my grandson, Walter. May his generation inherit all the natural beauty and biodiversity that my generation did.

It would be impossible to acknowledge the hundreds of birders, conservationists, and friends who shaped my understanding of the inextricable ties between plants and birds. And a great many people have taken me to their patches throughout the country, showing me how very much habitat work is being done on local, state, regional, and national levels, and why this work is so necessary.

I must mention one, Ali Sheehey, my go-to authority on California birds and habitats, who gave me helpful suggestions on the manuscript and prepared the list of native plant organizations for each state and province. I am in awe of her expertise, her willingness to help a friend in need, and her passionate commitment to living up to her high standards of conservation ethics.

Contents

· PART I ·

Creating Habitat

MORE THAN 50 MILLION North Americans feed birds, which is enjoyable for us and can be valuable for some popular species as well. But suet, sugar water, and birdseed provide food for only a fraction of our backyard birds, and our feeders don't offer a complete and balanced diet for any of them. We can see a much wider variety of birds, and support them much more comprehensively, when we add a good assortment of locally native plants to our landscaping.

This is a guide to some of the most important plants for supporting North American birds in the healthiest, most natural way possible.

PINE WARBLER

NORTHERN PARULA

Backyard Bounty

IMPROVING BACKYARD HABITAT to sustain birds does not need to *replace* bird feeding—a gratifying hobby that makes life a little easier for our backyard birds and can even save lives during severe winter weather. But even the best feeding stations can't match the importance of the right *plants* for bird welfare.

Plants produce seeds, fruits, nectar, and other essential foods. They host the caterpillars, aphids, and other insects almost all songbirds and a great many other birds need for protein; they also provide nesting and roosting sites and nesting materials. Many birds first discover feeders when they are drawn to a yard by an attractive tree or other conspicuous plant.

Bird-Plant Relationships

Some birds are inextricably bound to specific types of plants, and sometimes their names reflect that relationship, as with Pine Warblers, Oak and Juniper Titmice, Pinyon

Misnomers

Some plant references in bird names aren't very appropriate. In 1810, Alexander Wilson shot a brilliant warbler out of a magnolia tree in Mississippi and named it for the tree. But Magnolia Warblers nest in conifers far north of the range of magnolia trees and don't seem especially drawn to magnolias, either during spring or fall migration or on their wintering grounds in Central America and the Caribbean.

And a full 98 percent of all Palm Warblers breed in Canada's boreal forest, more than a thousand miles from the nearest palm trees. Palm Warblers winter in the Caribbean, along the Gulf Coast, in all of Florida, and along the southeastern Atlantic coast, so many do spend time near palm trees. But they forage mostly on the ground, not in trees, making the name inappropriate in any season.

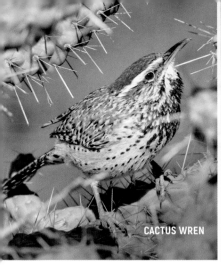

CACTUS WREN

FLORIDA SCRUB-JAY

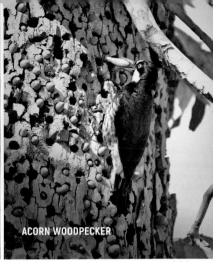

ACORN WOODPECKER

Jays, Cactus Wrens, and the two species of sage-grouse. Acorn Woodpeckers spend their lives near oaks, gathering and stashing away acorns in large, communal "granaries."

Plants may not be reflected in the name of North America's tiniest warbler, the Northern Parula, but in the Southeast it nests almost exclusively within clumps of Spanish moss, a bromeliad; in the Appalachians and northern forests, it nests within clumps of the *Usnea* lichens called "old man's beard."

Red-cockaded Woodpeckers of the Southeast nest in longleaf pines. They disappear as these pines are cut, even if the trees are replaced with other kinds of pines.

Kirtland's Warblers nest only on the ground beneath the lowest branches of young jack pine trees. As those trees age, they lose their bottom branches and can no longer shelter the warblers' ground nests. Jack pine cones open to release their seeds only following the high-intensity heat of

fires, so jack pine stands need to be burned periodically to allow new seedlings to take over and thus restore the warblers' nesting habitat.

Florida Scrub-Jays require scrub oaks. Baltimore Orioles once preferred to build

KIRTLAND'S WARBLER

JACK PINE CONE

RED CROSSBILL

PILEATED WOODPECKERS

AMERICAN
GOLDFINCH

their nests in elms, but as Dutch elm disease wiped out American elms, the orioles adapted to sycamores, maples, and other large trees.

Red Crossbills are very dependent on pine cones—spruce, tamarack, and other cones aren't nearly as attractive to them—while White-winged Crossbills feed on those other cones far more than they do on pine cones. Many populations of Red Crossbills wander from area to area as local pines produce bumper cone crops, even breeding in winter when pine seeds are abundant.

Although a handful of birds are extreme **specialists**, dependent on a single species of plant for food or nesting, most are less particular. Still, even some generalists do best around particular plants; here are some examples.

- Evening Grosbeaks are especially attracted to maple and boxelder seeds, and redpolls to birch seeds.

- Pileated Woodpeckers are drawn to aspens, because these softwoods are vulnerable to heart rot just as the trees reach an optimal girth for the birds to dig out large nesting and roosting cavities.

- American Goldfinches not only eat thistle and milkweed seeds but also incorporate these soft, downy seed fibers into their tightly woven nests.

Succession describes the process of change in natural communities, beginning with pioneer species and ultimately reaching a stable **climax** stage. Backyard landscaping can include plants from different stages of succession.

Getting Started

STARTING A BIRD GARDEN can be tricky. To begin with, species names can be most confusing. When the American Ornithologists' Union published the first *Check-List of North American Birds* in 1886, they included an English name and a Latin scientific name for each, to foster clear communication for both ornithologists and amateurs. Despite the many checklists and guidebooks published since, bird names are still hard to keep straight.

Plant names are even less standardized; in fact, botanists and horticulturists often use different vernacular names for the same species. For example, North America has no true cedar trees, which belong to the genus *Cedrus* and are native to the mountains of the western Himalayas and the Mediterranean region. Our

"cedars" belong to several different genera: *Calocedrus, Callitropsis, Juniperus,* and *Thuja.*

A great many plants are known by multiple names, and landscapers and greenhouses in the same state may use different names for the same species. Compounding those difficulties are the countless cultivars developed by horticulturists.

Advice on Local Species

This book lists each recommended plant's genus, along with one or more species representing some good choices for different parts of the country. There are usually a great many more possibilities than just those we included. State and local birding and gardening organizations can provide excellent lists of the best **locally native** species and varieties—meaning those that are native to your particular location, not just to your continent, state, or broader region—and they can warn about locally problematic species. (See page 250 for a list of North American native plant societies.)

Some local gardening stores may also have helpful suggestions. Make sure, however, that the people you talk to are aware of wildlife and ecological issues. A great many nonnative plants become **invasive**—that is, they grow so abundantly that they crowd out essential native plants while providing few or none of the benefits native plants do.

Some stores continue to sell such invasive exotics as purple loosestrife, multiflora rose, and black locust. Some even continue to recommend one dangerous exotic, heavenly bamboo (*Nandina*), saying that its red berries attract birds, even though those berries are toxic to birds!

ECOLOGICALLY HARMFUL INVASIVE PLANTS *NOT* TO INVITE INTO YOUR BACKYARD

PURPLE LOOSESTRIFE

MULTIFLORA ROSE

COMMON BUCKTHORN

ORIENTAL BITTERSWEET

JAPANESE KNOTWEED

HEAVENLY BAMBOO

Some Native Plants You Won't Find Here

A few wonderful native plants can be inappropriate in backyards for various reasons, and so they aren't included in this book.

Old-Growth Conifers

In California, a state filled with stunning natural wonders, sequoias and redwoods may be the most magnificent of all. The old-growth forests that both trees depend on provide vital habitat for Spotted Owls and Pileated Woodpeckers. Marbled Murrelets nest only on the branches of old-growth conifers, especially coast redwood.

Sequoia and coast redwoods grow very fast in their first decade, however, so neither is a good choice for yards even within the trees' natural ranges, unless the property is large and contiguous with old-growth forests. These trees must be planted far from any buildings, powerlines, or other infrastructure that could be damaged if they toppled.

The Saguaro Cactus

An icon of the Southwest, the saguaro is invaluable for birds in its native range, the Sonoran Desert of Mexico and southern Arizona, extending a bit into California. But saguaros grow extremely slowly at first, often taking 5 years or more to reach a height of 5 inches (13 cm). In places like Saguaro National Monument, where summer rainfall averages 16 or so inches (41 cm) a year, a saguaro takes 30 years to reach flowering size. Where rainfall averages only 9 inches (23 cm) per year, such as Organ Pipe National Monument, plants may not bloom for the first time until they are

75 years old. Several birds use large, mature saguaros for nesting, but, again, that can't happen until the cactus is many decades old.

Saguaros are declining dangerously, and it's critical that we plant them now to ensure that there are healthy mature plants well into the future. Young saguaros' value for birds is limited, however, and they require a great deal of care and attention to thrive. Supporting the organizations that are tirelessly working to protect this wonderful natural resource is an excellent alternative way for backyard bird gardeners to make a difference.

If your property can serve as a good site for a saguaro long into the future, these organizations will have tips on ethical sources for seeds and small plants and the information you'll need to grow your plant properly.

North American Classics

The American elm and American chestnut, both of extraordinary value for birds, are also critically endangered, in both cases because of diseases that have decimated them. Researchers are working hard to develop resistant cultivars. Supporting their work is important. As with groups trying to save saguaros, the organizations working to develop resistant elms and chestnuts can help you find good sources for the most resistant trees so far developed, and tips for helping them thrive.

Planning Your Bird Garden

OUR BACKYARDS will be the most valuable for the widest variety of birds when we take all four seasons into account in our planning, and when we consider how the plants themselves will change from one year to the next. Our human life-span averages much longer than that of our backyard songbirds, but it is much shorter than that of some of the plants in a good landscaping project. As more and more birds adapt to quality backyard habitat, we take on a responsibility to protect that habitat for the long haul.

Thinking Long Term

Some people are reluctant to plant oaks, walnuts, maples, and other trees that take decades to reach maturity. Keep in mind, however, that long before these trees start producing acorns, nuts, or seeds, or are large enough for bird nests or nest cavities, they're hosting vast numbers of insects critical for kinglets, warblers, and other insectivorous birds. Many fruit trees start producing fruit within a few years and, like other plants, host insects from the start.

So do make room for trees in your garden plan, despite the long-term commitment they represent.

Four-Season Support

As gardeners plan flower beds, they typically consider colors—beautifully compatible or contrasting—along with the sequence of bloom from early spring through late fall. Well-thought-out landscaping for birds has

Even when young, oaks and other long-lived trees are of enormous value to birds, attracting insects and producing nutritious buds.

Left: A Brown Creeper forages in winter bark to find eggs and pupae hidden in the crevices. Right: A Varied Thrush dines on chokecherries in winter.

aesthetic appeal, too, but it also embraces the full annual cycle, from winter through the following winter, of a variety of bird species.

Hard as it is to believe, trees and shrubs provide a great deal of insect food even when temperatures are double digits below zero, mostly in the form of eggs and pupae hidden in the crevices of bark. Many birds have neither the knowhow to find them nor the properly shaped bills to extract them, but chickadees and titmice, nuthatches, kinglets, and creepers do.

Woodpeckers feast on these same insects and also hack into the wood to extract larvae of wood-boring beetles. Downy Woodpeckers cannot dig deeply enough to reach many of those beetles within the trunk, but the downies often follow Pileated Woodpeckers, taking advantage of the holes left by the big guys to probe even deeper into the heartwood themselves.

Most berries ripen fairly quickly, but a few, such as chokecherries and staghorn sumac, start out bitter-tasting and then sweeten over the course of the winter. They provide invaluable food as other fruits and berries are depleted.

When you take the long view, choosing several fruiting trees and shrubs, you will be rewarded with fruit-eating birds over a much longer time span than if you stop with just one or two berry bushes.

Diverse and Appropriate Plants

The first thing most people think of when they hear the phrase "gardening for birds" is a hummingbird garden. Choosing one or two hummingbird flowers can be wonderful during the time those plants are in bloom, since many of the flowers that attract hummingbirds are beautiful and vivid. And even if you choose just one or two plant species, you'll almost certainly attract hummers as they blossom.

If you take the long view, however, you'll see these charming little sprites much more often. A beneficial progression might include:

- Willows or alders to provide insects and a bit of oozing sap for the first arrivals

- A variety of flowers to offer nectar and insect food through late spring and summer

- Plants that host aphids and other tiny insects, to encourage hummingbirds to nest nearby, especially if the hummers can find lichens and spider silk to use as nesting material

- Later-blooming flowers to offer quick meals during migration south in late summer and early fall

Selecting good individual plants is important, but selecting a variety is even more beneficial. The more diverse but locally appropriate your landscaping choices, the wider the variety of birds they'll attract over the longer span of time.

You can expand your target species to provide plants that support chickadees and titmice, warblers, wrens, finches, and more. As you do so, consider each additional bird's needs for nesting materials, nesting sites, roosting places, and of course food (both directly, from seeds, fruits, and nectar and indirectly, in the form of insects hosted by the plants). Your backyard bird numbers should increase noticeably.

See page 248 for a chart listing the favorite plants—for feeding, nesting, and nest materials—of many common birds.

Left: A Ruby-throated Hummingbird drinks alder sap in early spring. **Right:** A rubythroat nests where she can find the right construction materials, along with aphids and tiny insects to feed her babies.

Skip the Nonnatives

It was hard to limit a coast-to-coast list of plants to 100, and this book, intended to help you find new ways to invite birds to your yard, had to exclude some excellent choices for just about every locality. But even if we'd included 1,000 plants, we wouldn't recommend any nonnative species.

Some nonnative plants popular with landscapers, such as many fruit trees, are not particularly invasive and attract a lot of birds. Growing fruit trees for our own consumption may be rewarding for us, but we must be prepared to see birds taking literal bites out of "our" cherries or pears.

Fruit-eating birds are fairly indiscriminate, gravitating to nonnative buckthorn, Japanese honeysuckle, and *Nandina* berries as often as to native berries. This may seem like a good thing for the birds—in particular, the robin population in North America has surged as invasive fruit-bearing trees and shrubs have proliferated, providing abundant berries for the undiscriminating robins.

But even if the birds don't seem to taste a difference, native plants are far, far better, both for birds and the environment. How does that make sense? Birds looking for fast food are rather like most human consumers: they're not well informed about the sourcing and long-term implications of various ingredients. Some fruits that birds eat with apparent gusto, such as *Nandina* berries, turn out to be very harmful for the species eating them—damaging essential habitat, reducing nest success, or even being outright toxic.

JAPANESE HONEYSUCKLE

Close-Up on an Invasive

COMMON BUCKTHORN (*Rhamnus cathartica*) is an extremely tenacious shrub, often planted as a privacy hedge and once used in herbal medicine as a rather noxious purgative. Its toxicity is apparently much worse for mammals than birds—a great many bird species feed on the berries and don't suffer any digestive problems. Indeed, birds are the means by which buckthorn spreads, the birds "planting" buckthorn seeds in their droppings wherever they roam.

The plant sprouts vigorously and repeatedly from the root collar following cutting, girdling, or burning. Applying herbicide to newly cut stumps is a fairly effective control method, but seeds may stay viable in the soil for several years before sprouting, so getting rid of it requires repeated treatments and long-term monitoring of infested areas.

Meanwhile, birds fly about after feeding on buckthorn elsewhere, planting seeds as quickly as we can eradicate old plants.

The birds pay a cost for those meals. Studies show that birds nesting in buckthorn suffer more nest losses to predators than do birds nesting in native trees and shrubs. And because buckthorn is invasive, crowding out native plants, birds have fewer alternatives.

A 2020 Yale study found that the displacement of native plant communities by invasive plants such as buckthorn is a key cause of collapses in insect populations. Insect eggs and, especially, newly hatched larvae fuel spring migration as well as feeding many of our favorite nesting songbirds.

Native plants support 35 times as many North American insects as nonnative plants do, so even those native plants that have evolved to attract mammals or bees rather than birds are still vitally important for our birds.

Immigrants brought buckthorn to North America in the nineteenth century or possibly earlier; now it's firmly established, or "naturalized," throughout the northern and central states and much of Canada. It is especially invasive in the Great Lakes area.

Other Problem Plants

Some invasive exotics cause immeasurable harm to both the natural environment birds need and our own safety. During the Dustbowl in the 1930s, settlers unwittingly brought **buffelgrass** (*Cenchrus* or *Pennisetum*), native to Africa, Asia, and the Middle East, to arid parts of the United States, hoping it would support more cattle grazing. Then in the 1970s and '80s, buffelgrass was also widely planted for erosion control. It seemed like a good idea to some land managers—buffelgrass is prolific, quickly covering bare ground to hold soil in place, and it's tolerant of dry desert conditions.

Like many other invasive exotics, however, buffelgrass crowds out and competes with native desert plants for nutrients, water, and sunshine. Desert wildflowers that pop up in open spaces between larger plants, bursting into bloom immediately following monsoon rains, get elbowed out by this fast-spreading species.

And unlike well-spaced native desert plants, dense buffelgrass fuels massive fires and proliferates in the aftermath. Lightning has always ignited natural fires in the desert, but fire can't spread easily in natural Southwestern desert habitat, where sparse vegetation minimizes fuel and bare ground serves as a natural firebreak. Wherever buffelgrass fills natural gaps, it provides plenty of fuel to accelerate the fire's spread. Buffelgrass seeds germinate quickly after a fire, proliferating long before native vegetation can recover, making the next fire even more devastating.

Planted by settlers, buffelgrass has caused a cascade of problems in North American deserts.

Multiflora rose (*Rosa multiflora*) is another plant once touted by land managers and even state departments of natural resources as a source of food for wildlife; now it's considered a serious invasive problem, crowding out the native plants that field and grassland birds need in vulnerable habitats.

Go Locally Native

When choosing plants, whether you want to help birds or simply make your property lovelier, the wisest choices are not just plants native to the continent but those species and varieties that are locally native—native to the area in your state where you're planting them. These are the plants that will most easily thrive in your local climate, minimizing the need for supplemental water, fertilizer, and protection from weather extremes. They're also the plants associated with and fostering the largest variety of local insects, the species most beneficial to your birds.

. . . BUT AVOID INVASIVE LOCALS

Ironically, even some locally native plants have become invasive due to mismanagement. **Mesquite** (*Prosopis* spp.) is an incredibly important plant in the arid Southwest—a legume able to enrich desert soils with nitrogen. Birds feed on its seeds and nest in its sheltering branches, and it is a primary source of food for the beautiful Gambel's Quail. But thanks to human-caused factors—including overgrazing, the increasing temperatures and more frequent droughts associated with climate change, and fire suppression—mesquites are outcompeting or shading out many plants, reducing the diversity necessary in any healthy ecosystem.

Now mesquite is listed among the 20 most significant weeds in the United States and is the most common and widely spread pest plant in Texas, where about 25 percent of grasslands are infested. All mesquites are listed as noxious weeds in Florida.

CACTUS WREN ON MESQUITE

BLACK LOCUST

The **black locust** (*Robinia pseudoacacia*) was once fairly restricted in range, even though it grows in dense stands because new growth sprouts from the root systems. It's become invasive in Northern California and much of the West, New England, and the Midwest, because those dense stands crowd out locally native species. When black locust proliferates in grassland, oak savanna, and other open habitats, it competes for nutrients, shades large swaths of sun-loving vegetation, and converts what had been climax open habitat into forest.

Forests are vitally important, of course, but grassland and savanna ecosystems are, too, and they've been decreasing in size thanks to development, overgrazing, and other issues. Black locust exacerbates their loss, endangering birds such as Prairie Warblers and other wildlife that require true grassland, scrub, and savanna habitat.

So What *Do* We Plant?

A book of this nature cannot possibly list all the best choices for every yard. The plants listed here, all native to the United States and Canada, are good possibilities to start with, but state and local native plant organizations and birding clubs should be able to provide you with invaluable advice relevant to your local situation. A native plant society for each state and province is listed on page 250; online searches and local gardeners may help you find more sources for local information.

Birdscaping Your Property

CREATING A WELCOMING YARD means thinking about time as well as space, and taking a good look at the bird-friendly features you might provide.

Meeting Seasonal Needs

As you look through the plant choices in this book, think about the birds you hope to attract throughout the year, and the plants that will best suit their needs.

Winter Browsers

- Do waxwings, Pine Grosbeaks, robins and thrushes, and other berry-eating species winter near you?

- How about grouse and other birds that feed on catkins and buds?

- Do you have any thick conifers to provide shelter during blizzards and ice storms?

- Are there large shade trees into which woodpeckers can carve roost cavities?

Spring Nesters

- As winter releases its hold, willows often provide the first food for early spring migrants. Which flowers open first in your area?

- Will there be berries for catbirds, thrashers, robins, thrushes, orioles, and other fruit lovers?

- Are there vines and shrubs to provide cover for nesting birds?

Hummers, Singers, and Travelers

- Hummingbirds and just about all songbirds feed insects to their young. Do you have a good assortment of plants that host an abundance of insects?

- As flycatchers, kinglets, warblers, and other insectivores pass through in spring and fall, do you have plants that support plenty of insects to feed them?

- As summer wanes, are there good sources of seeds and berries as well as insects to sustain migrating birds?

NORTHERN CARDINAL

AMERICAN ROBIN

WHITE-CROWNED SPARROW

Taking a Bird's-Eye View

As you see how well native plants provide for birds, you may want to grow even more of them, little by little reducing the amount of space devoted to lawn, which offers native birds virtually no benefits. You may also find areas of your yard where neatness isn't important, where tangles of shrubs and brush piles can provide nesting areas and, during migration, cover for visiting songbirds when hawks fly over.

Think long term about your landscape. As time goes by and trees die, you may want to leave them standing for a few years (if they don't pose a danger to people or buildings) to provide insects and cavities for woodpeckers and good lookout perches for flycatchers and waxwings. Once they do topple, edge your garden beds with the fallen limbs and trunks to offer more dining opportunities for woodpeckers.

Water: At Least as Vital as Food

Just about anywhere, water features and birdbaths are extremely attractive for birds. Indeed, the best opportunities for closeup photography of warblers and other nonfeeder birds are often at birdbaths and small backyard ponds. To provide these ethically in areas of water shortages, you must be careful to follow the spirit as well as the letter of local water conservation ordinances.

Top: Bluebirds perch on snags to survey the ground for insects and may nest in woodpecker cavities. **Bottom:** This pair of Eastern Bluebirds is making the most of a backyard birdbath.

Scrub Those Birdbaths

No matter where you live, you must be committed to cleaning birdbaths every three or four days to ensure that there isn't enough time for mosquito eggs to hatch. Stagnant water is a primary breeding source of the specific mosquitoes that spread West Nile virus and other diseases that harm us as well as birds.

When maintained properly, hosing down the birdbaths while scrubbing them with a stiff brush is enough. Never put anything toxic in the water to control plant growth.

Keep Birds Safe in Your Yard

LANDSCAPING FOR BIRDS is a vital foundational step in providing for birds, but it must not be the only step.

Making sure your birdbaths are clean and the water nontoxic is just one way to ensure the safety of the birds you invite to your yard. People who set out birdbaths or feeders or maintain backyard habitat to attract birds have a moral obligation to take care that they're not inviting birds to their deaths.

Keep Cats Indoors

Occasionally a Cooper's Hawk or a fox will kill birds in our yards. These wild predators are part of the ecosystems to which birds are adapted. Domestic cats, however, are not part of any natural system in North America. They may be "natural" in the sense that they kill birds and other animals by instinct, but genuinely natural predators are subject to disease, predation, and other forces that keep their numbers in balance. When natural predators deplete local prey populations, they move on or starve.

In contrast, pet cats and those supported by feral cat organizations are fed and given at least some veterinary care to prevent death from diseases and injuries. These protections keep domesticated cat numbers much higher than any natural predator populations could sustain, in effect making cats subsidized killers. This is why so many bird conservation organizations work toward passage of "cats-indoors" ordinances.

Now that trap-neuter-release programs protecting feral cats have been underway for more than a decade, there is substantial evidence that, contrary to the assurances of proponents, they've not reduced feral cat numbers at all. Cats kill on the order of a billion birds in the United States alone every year.

Do everything you can to keep outdoor cats away from your property, and support local cats-indoors ordinances.

Make Window Glass Visible

Window glass is another mass murderer of birds, killing roughly the same number every year that cats do. There are many ways to make your windows more visible to birds, including exterior screening, "Zen wind curtains" (lengths of paracord, spaced no more than 4 inches [10 cm] apart, hung from a dowel or other support), and stickers on the outside of the glass, spaced no more than 4 inches (10 cm) apart.

Please do everything you can to protect your backyard birds from your windows.

Go Wild

As more and more people appreciate the benefits of native habitat and the environmental costs of maintaining lawns, more and more cities and towns are allowing people to let their yards grow wild. That may be the best solution of all, for you and the birds you enjoy.

Avoid Pesticides and Fertilizers

No pesticide is "EPA approved." The Environmental Protection Agency registers pesticides if there is no documented and significant evidence that they cause harm, or if the manufacturer can make a case that the benefits outweigh the harms. There is, however, little enforcement to ensure that pesticides are limited to their prescribed uses, and there are no regulations requiring that pesticides be tested for their effects on songbirds.

Since the late 1980s, field testing to determine whether a chemical might cause unexpected environmental consequences is no longer required for registration. And almost no research has been conducted on the effects of multiple pesticides used together, even though pesticides are often applied in complex mixtures and may cause far worse problems in combination than alone.

If you must resort to herbicide use to eliminate a particularly persistent invasive plant, spot-spray it. If you're having a serious insect problem in your garden that you really can't resolve without insecticide applications, exclude birds from the area with bird netting erected around sturdy supports to keep it taut so birds won't become entangled.

Fertilizer runoff is a scourge in lakes, rivers, and streams. If we plant only locally native species, adapted to local soil and rainfall conditions, they'll require less water and fewer fertilizer applications. Please remember that lawn care companies develop formulas for regions, not specific localities, and many use the same applications whether a lawn is already lush or really could benefit from fertilizer, and whether your area is in the midst of a drought or expecting rain the very next day.

They use the exact same insecticides, applied over every square inch of lawn, regardless of whether your yard has ever had even one cutworm, and they apply the exact same herbicides over every square inch of lawn whether you have six dandelions or six bazillion.

For the Love of Birds

MANY BIRDWATCHERS, including the author of this book, pay much less attention to plants than to the birds we train our binoculars and cameras on. But the more aware we are of plants as part of the ecological communities associated with different kinds of birds, the more informed we can be not only about our own backyards but also about local, state, and national issues regarding ecology and conservation.

Whether your property is a small residential lot in a major city, a large suburban backyard, a vast rural acreage, on the shoreline, or anything else, plant it with beneficial, locally native vegetation. Keep cats indoors, make your windows bird safe, and minimize or eliminate pesticides and fertilizers to benefit the local and migrating birds you love.

Remember, *to love* is an active verb. The birds who enrich our lives so very much deserve our love and our active protection.

TUFTED TITMOUSE

Bird-Attracting Features of Different Plants

Birds rely on different plants for a variety of resources that include not only food (buds, seeds, fruit, nectar, insects) but also housing, shelter, nest materials, and more. Throughout this book, the following icons will indicate special features that each plant offers.

BEES
Is also valuable to bees

BERRIES, FRUIT
Produces berries or fruits that are especially nutritious for birds

BUTTERFLIES
Is also valuable to butterflies

CATERPILLARS
Hosts exceptional numbers of butterfly and moth larvae, the main source of protein for a great many songbirds

CATKINS
Produces catkins with special value for insectivores, and for birds in general in late winter and early spring

CAVITY
Preferred by birds that build nesting holes

CONES
Produces cones with nutrient-rich seeds, important food for many bird species

INSECTS
Attracts aphids and other small insects preferred by small fly-catching birds

MAST
Produces acorns or other nuts critical for some birds

NECTAR
Produces nectar that is especially accessible to hummingbirds, orioles, and other birds

NESTING/ROOSTING
Provides safe, sheltered spots for birds to nest and **roost** (spend their inactive hours)

SAP
Has flowing, accessible sap in spring, important for sapsuckers and many smaller early spring migrants that feed on the sap and on the insects attracted to it

SEEDS
Produces seeds that are especially nutritious and easy for birds to access and eat

WARNING
Some plants that provide excellent sources of food or shelter for birds are not good choices in backyards for various reasons—growing too large, for example. In addition, plants that are critically important in one part of the continent may cause problems in other areas.

WINTER BUDS
Produces nutritious buds that are eaten (especially in winter) by grouse and other birds with specialized digestive systems

PART II

Plants That Support Birds

LONG BEFORE THERE WERE CHICKENS, eggs, or philosophers wondering which came first, there were plants creating the very oxygen every animal requires. The 10,000 or so species of birds on Earth may seem like a lot until we consider that there are close to 400,000 plant species. We name many large biomes by the dominant plant type ("northern coniferous forest," "oak savanna," or "eastern hardwood forest"), but every natural habitat includes a wide variety of other plants, too.

Let's look at some of the most important plants supporting North American birds.

CONIFERS

Conifers are woody plants that produce their seeds in cones. Although they are often called "evergreens," some conifers lose their needles seasonally. Many grow as shrubs as well as trees and provide food and shelter for many birds. Some birds are tied essentially to conifers, from Marbled Murrelets nesting in coastal old-growth conifers to Red Crossbills that take the vast majority of their food from pine cones.

Many conifers ooze droplets of sap from the tips of needles, buds, and branches, where insects and hummingbirds feed; native conifers also harbor a wealth of insects that provide food for birds.

Bald Cypress
Taxodium

Cedar, Juniper
Juniperus, Thuja, Chamaecyparis

Cypress
Hesperocyparis, formerly *Cupressus*

Douglas-fir
Pseudotsuga

Fir
Abies

Hemlock
Tsuga

Pine
Pinus

Spruce
Picea

Tamarack, Larch
Larix

1 Bald Cypress

Taxodium

Like other deciduous conifers, bald and pond cypress trees produce cones but drop their needlelike leaves every winter. Ducks, turkeys, and songbirds feed on the seeds and on insects in the trees. Colonies of herons, egrets, ibises, and other wading birds often nest in clusters of cypress trees.

Two extinct birds were closely associated with this species. The Ivory-billed Woodpecker once lived in old-growth swamps characterized by bald cypress and tupelo. The Carolina Parakeet fed heavily on bald cypress seeds and was a primary disseminator of seeds far beyond the swamps where the parent trees were rooted.

continued on next page

NATIVE RANGE

USES
- Wetland restoration
- Erosion control
- Shade tree

EXPOSURE: Sun

SOIL MOISTURE: Average to wet, including submerged

MOST USEFUL SEASON(S): Year-round

COLOR(S): Green

MAXIMUM HEIGHT: 150 feet (46 m) in the wild

RECOMMENDED SPECIES

Taxonomists classify cypresses in *Taxodium* as one, two, or three species. The bald cypress (*T. distichum*), the state tree of Louisiana, is native to the southeastern United States from Delaware to Texas, and especially from Louisiana up the Mississippi River to southern Indiana. This is the cypress usually sold in garden stores. It must be near water to develop cypress knees (root appendages that protrude around the tree above the waterline or ground level in irregular conical shapes), but it grows well, without those knees, in average soil conditions in its natural range.

The pond cypress (*T. ascendens*) is found within the bald cypress's range, along the southeastern coastal plain from North Carolina to Louisiana, in still blackwater rivers, ponds, and swamps. The Montezuma cypress (*T. mucronatum*) is native to Mexico and Guatemala, occurring in the United States only in the Lower Rio Grande Valley.

WHITE IBIS

2 Cedar, Juniper

Juniperus, Thuja, Chamaecyparis

INVASIVE; ATTRACT DEER

As popular with landscapers as with birds, cedars and junipers are attractive evergreen trees and shrubs. Their dense branches shelter wintering birds, including owls, and provide nesting as well as roosting shelter for such species as Chipping and Song Sparrows, robins, and mockingbirds. Their cones provide abundant and nutritious food for many species.

The blue "berries" on junipers and redcedars are actually tiny female cones: The scales are consolidated into what looks like berry skin. Many fruit-eating birds eat them, including American Robin, Townsend's Solitaire, Mountain Bluebird, Clark's Nutcracker, Steller's Jay, and Phainopepla. The Cedar Waxwing is named for its concentrations in winter where redcedars are abundant. In cold weather when insects aren't available, Yellow-rumped Warblers and Tree Swallows may descend en masse into junipers both for shelter and to feed on the berries.

continued on next page

NATIVE RANGE

USES
- Hedgerow
- Windbreak
- Ornamental

EXPOSURE: Sun to shade

SOIL MOISTURE: Dry to wet, depending on species

MOST USEFUL SEASON(S): Year-round

COLOR(S): Shades of green

MAXIMUM HEIGHT: 125 feet (38 m); many species are much more shrubby

Our North American species include eastern redcedar and Rocky Mountain juniper in the genus *Juniperus*, eastern and northern white-cedar and western redcedar in *Thuja*, and the fairly rare Atlantic white-cedar and Port Orford cedar or Lawson's cypress in *Chamaecyparis*. These genera also include nonnative species. Western juniper (*J. occidentalis*) and some other native juniper species in drier habitats of the Great Plains and the West have become a serious ecological problem because they grow so densely as late-stage successional species. Unless occasional fires, which were once a natural occurrence, keep them in check, they end up crowding out other native vegetation. Fire suppression has allowed junipers to take over essential habitat for the Greater Sage-Grouse, Black-capped Vireo, Golden-cheeked Warbler, Green-tailed Towhee, Brewer's Sparrow, and other species. These birds depend on native grasses, sagebrush, scrub oaks, or other plants characteristic of early-successional habitat where intermittent fires provided a natural

CEDAR WAXWING

BLACK-CAPPED VIREO

balance. Planting backyard junipers within several miles of vulnerable grassland, sagebrush, or scrub habitat will foster juniper encroachment because birds "plant" their seeds far from where they eat them.

RECOMMENDED SPECIES

Local nurseries and native plant gardeners may have suggestions about good locally native choices, as well as information about whether junipers are a good choice in your area. Within their ranges, California juniper (*Juniperus californica*), Rocky Mountain juniper (*J. scopulorum*), eastern redcedar (*J. virginiana*), and northern white-cedar (*Thuja occidentalis*) are all excellent for birds, as are other locally native species. Northern white-cedar is very vulnerable to deer; when attracted to it, the deer may munch on your other plants as well.

NORTHERN WHITE-CEDAR

Also Known As . . .

Americans use the words "cedar," "juniper," and "arborvitae" fairly interchangeably. Many horticulturists and botanists consider Old World plants belonging to the genus *Cedrus* to be the only true cedars, so they often use "redcedar," "white-cedar," and similar variations to refer to North American species. When you consider that the northern white-cedar is also called the Atlantic redcedar, however, this hardly clears up matters, and makes finding locally native species especially confusing.

3 Cypress

Hesperocyparis, formerly *Cupressus*

Dense foliage makes cypress trees very useful for birds to roost in and shelter from weather and predators. The upper branches are so dense that they can even provide safe perches for North America's largest flying bird, the California Condor.

Cypress seed cones often stay tightly closed until after a fire, when new seedlings quickly sprout. Red-breasted Nuthatches feed on the seeds in the cones, and woodpeckers and other insectivores feed on larvae hosted by cypress.

RECOMMENDED SPECIES

North America's cypress trees were until recently placed with Old World cypress trees in *Cupressus.* Found only in the far West north to British Columbia and in the Southwest through Mexico and Central America, most cypress species have very restricted and local ranges.

USES
- Ornamental
- Shade tree
- Hedgerow
- Windbreak

EXPOSURE: Sun

SOIL MOISTURE: Well drained

MOST USEFUL SEASON(S): Year-round

COLOR(S): Evergreen

MAXIMUM HEIGHT: 130 feet (40 m)

NATIVE RANGE

Several California species are **endemic** to parts of the state, meaning that they are native and found only in limited areas. These species include the beautiful and popular Monterey cypress (*Hesperocyparis macrocarpa*), which is considered endangered within its small natural range even as people grow it as an exotic in many places throughout the world. The Arizona cypress (*H. arizonica*) ranges through southern California, Arizona, Utah, and southwestern New Mexico, with a few populations in southern Nevada and the Chisos Mountains in west Texas.

Because cypress trees produce large quantities of pollen, they are probably not good choices for people with allergies or for plantings in dense neighborhoods.

Atop a Monterey cypress, a California Condor dries the dew off its feathers in the early morning sunlight.

4 Douglas-fir

Pseudotsuga

A popular landscaping tree in the West, the handsome Douglas-fir (which is not a true fir—those belong to the genus *Abies*) provides abundant food, roosting, and nesting for birds. Many species feed on the seeds, including Dark-eyed Juncos; Song, White-crowned, and Golden-crowned Sparrows; Pine Siskins; Purple Finches; and White-winged Crossbills. Sooty and Dusky Grouse eat the needles.

A wide variety of birds, from woodpeckers to chickadees and warblers, feed on the larvae of white-pine

SOOTY GROUSE

WHITE-WINGED CROSSBILL

USES
• Shade tree

EXPOSURE: Part or full shade when young

SOIL MOISTURE: Dry to moist, but must be well drained

MOST USEFUL SEASON(S): Year-round

COLOR(S): Evergreen

MAXIMUM HEIGHT: 250 feet (76 m)

NATIVE RANGE

butterfly and various moths, which Douglas-firs host, as well as aphids and other insects. Woodpeckers excavate cavities in the trunk and larger limbs. Those cavities and the tree's dense branches provide nesting and roosting for a wide variety of other birds as well.

The coastal subspecies of Douglas-fir is an essential component of old-growth in the Pacific rainforest. Hermit Warblers often feed, court, and nest in the high branches of Douglas-fir.

RECOMMENDED SPECIES

Human landscapers can't grow a climax forest from scratch within one lifetime, but even young Douglas-firs (*Pseudotsuga menziesii*) will provide food and shelter for a wide variety of birds and other wildlife. As a climax tree, seedlings and tiny saplings will need some shade, but they can thrive in full sun as they grow. In dense stands, most Douglas-firs lose their lower branches as they get older but hold onto them better in full sun. They don't reach full height except in old-growth forests.

Close Connection

The endangered specialist Spotted Owl is tightly associated with Douglas-fir climax forests, focusing much of its hunting on flying squirrels and other arboreal rodents, including red tree voles. These voles are found almost exclusively in old Douglas-firs, nesting in the foliage and eating the needles.

As younger successional trees fill in after logging, Spotted Owls can't compete with the more aggressive Barred Owls, which as generalists take a wider range of prey and so are better adapted to younger forests.

SPOTTED OWL

VEERY

5

Fir

Abies

Beautiful and fragrant, firs are splendid trees, and balsam fir (*Abies balsamea*) is considered a keystone in the boreal forest. Some grouse eat fir buds and needles in winter, and as with other conifers, birds from juncos to small owls take shelter in the dense branches at night and during storms.

Balsam is an important nesting tree for such lovely birds as Veeries, Blackpoll Warblers, and Rose-breasted Grosbeaks, and it is the primary nesting tree for the endangered Bicknell's Thrush.

Because balsams are fairly short lived but remain standing for years as their branches lose their needles, they often host pale greenish "old man's beard" lichens (*Usnea* spp.) in their branches. The shrublike lichens are not parasitic and don't harm the trees in which they grow. But since they thrive where the upper branches have died, letting in light for photosynthesis, people sometimes mistakenly think lichens are what caused a fir's death.

The cones of firs stand vertically like candles. Many birds, including White-winged Crossbills and Pine Siskins, eat

USES
- Reforestation
- Hedgerow

EXPOSURE: Sun to shade

SOIL MOISTURE: Moist but well drained

MOST USEFUL SEASON(S): Year-round

COLOR(S): Evergreen

MAXIMUM HEIGHT: 230 feet (70 m)

NATIVE RANGE

the seeds from those cones. As the cones mature, their scales start falling away, releasing winged seeds even as the cones themselves remain on the tree.

Seed-eating birds can thrive in "good mast years" when cones are most abundant. Ironically, however, those years are very hard on birds that nest in fir branches, particularly Bicknell's Thrush, because so many red squirrels gravitate to the cone-laden trees. These adorable little rodents are mainly interested in collecting cones, but they get needed protein from eating any eggs or nestlings they encounter.

Commercially, firs are more valuable as wood pulp than as lumber because their soft wood rots quickly, although they are heavily harvested as Christmas trees while still young.

Spruce budworm (*Choristoneura* spp.) is more likely to attack balsam fir than spruces. These native insects are an economic problem in commercial forests, but they provide an important food source for native birds feeding young, especially the beautiful Blackburnian and Cape May Warblers. The dramatic decline of the Evening Grosbeak population can be traced in part to spruce budworm eradication programs.

RUFFED GROUSE

EVENING GROSBEAK

continued on next page

RECOMMENDED SPECIES

Firs are not very long lived, and most require consistently humid air in order to thrive. The balsam fir (*Abies balsamea*) does well at edges or within woodlands, where layers of fallen leaves and needles hold soil moisture and the proximity of other trees keeps the air moist.

Fraser fir (*A. fraseri*), the only fir endemic to the temperate rainforest of the southern Appalachian Mountains, is raised on tree farms for the Christmas tree trade. It is badly endangered in its natural range, however, due to an invasive exotic insect, the balsam woolly adelgid (*Adelges piceae*). Fraser fir and the native firs in the West, primarily grand fir (*Abies grandis*), Rocky Mountain fir (*A. lasiocarpa*), and white fir (*A. concolor*), are found at higher elevations.

Grand fir is considered the tallest fir in the world, sometimes reaching heights of 230 feet (70 m). Other firs are considerably shorter.

BLACK-CAPPED CHICKADEE

6 Hemlock

Tsuga

YELLOW-BELLIED SAPSUCKERS

Handsome medium to large conifers, hemlocks thrive in moist, cool temperate areas with high rainfall, cool summers, and little or no water stress. They are also adapted to cope with heavy winter snowfall and tolerate ice storms better than most other trees. They are not toxic; they were given the name because their crushed foliage smells a bit like the unrelated poisonous plant credited with killing Socrates. Landscapers appreciate that unlike most conifers, hemlocks prefer partial shade and can even thrive in full shade.

The dense branches provide excellent cover for a wide variety of roosting and nesting birds. Ruffed Grouse and Great Horned Owls frequently roost in the branches, especially in winter. Blue-headed Vireos,

continued on next page

Winter Wrens, a variety of beautiful warblers (including Blackburnian, Magnolia, and Black-throated Green), and both Black-capped and Boreal Chickadees nest and feed on insects in these conifers.

Hemlocks are very long lived, making the trunk and large limbs excellent for excavating nest cavities for a variety of woodpeckers, from Yellow-bellied Sapsuckers to Pileated Woodpeckers. Small owls then use these cavities as nesting sites. Boreal Chickadees, White-winged Crossbills, and many other finches and songbirds feed on the seed cones.

RECOMMENDED SPECIES

Eastern or Canadian hemlock (*Tsuga canadensis*), the state tree of Pennsylvania, grows well in shade, tolerates a lot of pruning, and can be very long lived. The Carolina hemlock (*T. caroliniana*) is native only in southwest Virginia, western North Carolina, northwest South Carolina, extreme northeast Georgia, and eastern Tennessee, on rocky slopes at elevations of 2,300 to 3,900 feet (700 to 1,190 m). Western hemlock (*T. heterophylla*) is an integral part of the Pacific Northwest forests and the Coastal Ranges.

An invasive insect from Asia, the hemlock woolly adelgid (*Adelges tsugae*), is responsible for a serious decline in North American hemlocks.

BLUE-HEADED VIREO

BLACK-THROATED GREEN WARBLER

HEMLOCK

NATIVE RANGE

USES
- Reforestation
- Ornamental

EXPOSURE: Full sun to full shade

SOIL MOISTURE: Consistently moist but well drained

MOST USEFUL SEASON(S): Year-round

COLOR(S): Evergreen

MAXIMUM HEIGHT: 150 feet (46 m)

CLARK'S NUTCRACKER

7 Pine

Pinus

Many people call all conifers by the generic name "pine trees," but they are just one subset of a great many conifer species—and birds know the difference. There are about 126 species of pines in the world, all belonging to the genus *Pinus*, which is divided into two subgenera: white or soft pines, with up to five needles per bunch; and red or hard pines, with two or three needles per bunch.

Fully half of the diet of Red Crossbills, Clark's Nutcrackers, and White-headed Woodpeckers are pine seeds. Dusky, Sooty, Spruce, and Sharp-tailed Grouse eat pine needles. A great many more species enjoy the smorgasbord of insect food provided by pines—the larvae of 191 native insect species are associated with eastern white pine alone.

Many migratory warblers feed on these insects by day and take shelter in the dense branches during bad weather and at night when stopping over during their journey. A great many birds nest or roost in the dense branches of pines or in cavities.

continued on next page

Left: The Cassia Crossbill is tightly associated with the Rocky Mountain lodgepole pine.
Right: A White-headed Woodpecker plucks a seed from a pine cone.

RECOMMENDED SPECIES

There are dozens of species of native pine trees in the United States and Canada, which could complicate selecting species for your property. Pines are fairly popular ornamental trees, however, so people at local bird and garden clubs and responsible gardening centers should have good suggestions for locally native pines that suit your needs.

Many birds are drawn to pines in general; Red Crossbills are an example. However, some Red Crossbill subspecies, which may eventually be split into their own species, have more specific pine needs. One that already has been split, the Cassia Crossbill (found only in Idaho's South Hills and Albion Mountains in Cassia County), feeds particularly on the Rocky Mountain lodgepole pine (*Pinus contorta* var. *latifolia*).

If you live within the nesting range of vulnerable bird species that need specific pines, consider planting one of those in your backyard habitat. For example, White-headed Woodpeckers are tightly associated with ponderosa pines (*P. ponderosa*), but in the southern part of the woodpecker's range, they may also be found nesting and feeding in Jeffrey (*P. jeffreyi*), sugar (*P. lambertiana*), and Coulter (*P. coulteri*) pines. Steller's Jays within the range of sugar pines hoard a great many of their

USES
- Reforestation
- Shade tree
- Ornamental
- Edible seeds

EXPOSURE: Full sun (a few species tolerate part shade)

SOIL MOISTURE: Moist, well drained

MOST USEFUL SEASON(S): Year-round

COLOR(S): Evergreen

MAXIMUM HEIGHT: 250 feet (76 m)

NATIVE RANGE

seeds after hammering the cones with their beaks and collecting the seeds that fall out.

Red-cockaded Woodpeckers nest only in longleaf pines (*P. palustris*), and Kirtland's Warblers nest only on the ground beneath young jack pines (*P. banksiana*). Pinyon Jays feed primarily on the nutlike seeds of the several species of pinyon pines (such as *P. monophylla* and *P. edulis*). Pinyon and Mexican Jays cache more nuts than they usually need, leaving some that will grow into new pinyon pines.

BALD EAGLE

Close Connection
Bald Eagles in the East strongly prefer to build their long-lasting nests in white pines (*Pinus strobus*). As eagles become more abundant, they are even nesting in some towns and cities—one pair has nested for at least a decade in a white pine on the edge of the playing fields and parking lot of a local high school in Duluth, Minnesota. It would be overly optimistic to plant a white pine in an urban center specifically to attract nesting Bald Eagles, but a great many more common birds will certainly take advantage.

8 Spruce
Picea

Like other conifers, spruces provide shelter for roosting and nesting birds and cones for seed-eating birds, especially Pine Siskins and White-winged Crossbills. Some grouse eat the needles and buds. Black-throated Green Warblers and Pileated Woodpeckers do much of their foraging in spruces.

This is an important tree in the breeding habitat of a wide variety of birds, including Spruce Grouse, Northern Saw-whet Owls, Olive-sided and Yellow-bellied Flycatchers, Canada Jays, Golden-crowned Kinglets, a host of warblers, White-throated Sparrows, and Evening Grosbeaks.

Moths with larvae called spruce budworms (*Choristoneura* spp.) have cyclical population surges, as do some birds, such as Evening Grosbeaks, that depend heavily on spruce budworm to feed their young.

Pesticides controlling spruce budworm aren't the whole reason for bird population declines. Changes in forest management in northern forests may also have contributed to the recent significant decline in Evening Grosbeaks. For example, more frequent logging prevents

USES
- Reforestation
- Windbreak
- Hedgerow
- Ornamental

EXPOSURE: Sun and partial sun

SOIL MOISTURE: Average

MOST USEFUL SEASON(S): Year-round

COLOR(S): Evergreen

MAXIMUM HEIGHT: 200 feet (61 m)

NATIVE RANGE

SPRUCE GROUSE

OLIVE-SIDED FLYCATCHER

hardwoods from getting established. This has a negative effect on Evening Grosbeaks, who feed heavily on maple and boxelder seeds.

RECOMMENDED SPECIES

Although Norway spruce (*Picea abies*) has been extremely popular with landscapers for well over a century, it's exotic everywhere in North America and invasive in the northern half of the United States. And blue spruce (*P. pungens*), the state tree of Colorado, has been widely planted and "naturalized" in areas well beyond its native range in New Mexico through Colorado and Utah to Wyoming. Locally native spruces are wiser choices.

White spruce (*P. glauca*), the provincial tree of Manitoba and state tree of South Dakota, reaches farther north than any other tree species in North America. In the far north it grows in single-species stands, as well as mixed with black spruce and tamarack, on the tree line at the edge of the Arctic tundra. White spruce must be in a stage of winter dormancy to survive extreme cold, but when dormant, the buds can survive temperatures as low as −94°F (−70°C).

Black spruce (*P. mariana*), the provincial tree of Newfoundland and Labrador, tolerates wet conditions and is associated with tamaracks in

continued on next page

northern bogs. Red spruce (*P. rubens*), the provincial tree of Nova Scotia, is an important timber tree in the Adirondacks and Appalachians. It's extremely vulnerable to acid rain.

Where more than one species is locally native, sometimes one choice is better in upland areas, and another where soils are wetter. For example, in northern forests, white spruce is better in drier habitats, black spruce in boggier places. Local bird conservation and garden groups focused on native plants will be able to suggest the best locally native spruces for your yard.

NORTHERN SAW-WHET OWL

CANADA JAY

9 Tamarack, Larch

Larix

People often use the words "conifer" and "evergreen" interchangeably, but tamaracks and larches are non-evergreen conifers. Their needles turn a gorgeous golden yellow in autumn, easily distinguishable after most deciduous trees have lost their leaves, and then the needles drop, leaving the trees as bare as maples and aspens for the winter. Young cones on tamaracks look like lovely pink flowers; older cones are brown and may remain on the trees for years after their seeds are gone.

The seeds of tamaracks and the two western larches provide an important food source for Pine Siskins, Common Redpolls, and White-winged Crossbills. Grouse feed on the needlelike leaves (especially on new growth in spring) and buds. White-throated and Song Sparrows, Veeries, Scarlet Tanagers, Common Yellowthroats, and Nashville Warblers are associated with tamarack forests in summer.

continued on next page

NATIVE RANGE

USES
- Ornamental
- Fall color

EXPOSURE: Full sun

SOIL MOISTURE: Moist, well drained

MOST USEFUL SEASON(S): Year-round

COLOR(S): Green, turning yellow in fall

MAXIMUM HEIGHT: 200 feet (61 m)

Top: Common Redpolls are one of many birds that feed heavily on tamarack seeds. **Bottom:** In winter and early spring, Ruffed Grouse will browse for tamarack buds and new growth.

RECOMMENDED SPECIES

Tamaracks and larches are extremely cold-tolerant, so they occur at the Arctic tree line at the very edge of the tundra. Tamaracks can survive and even thrive down to −85°F (−65°C). All three North American species—tamarack (*Larix laricina*), western larch (*L. occidentalis*), and subalpine larch (*L. lyallii*)—are extremely intolerant of shade and air pollution. They grow better in more naturalized settings but can do well if your property borders woodlands.

BROADLEAF TREES

As buds open in spring, tiny caterpillars emerge to feed on soft new leaves, providing the main source of food for migrating songbirds. The vast number and variety of insects associated with North America's broadleaf trees are critical for birds, and those trees provide an abundance of other food items such as acorns, fruits, nectar, and sap, to say nothing of essential roosting and nesting sites.

Deciduous trees usually dominate our landscaping plans; wise selections can support birds for many decades while adding beauty and joy to our lives.

Alder *Alnus*	**Desert Willow** *Chilopsis*	**Oak** *Quercus*
Aspen, Cottonwood *Populus*	**Hackberry** *Celtis*	**Redbud** *Cercis*
Basswood *Tilia*	**Hickory, Pecan** *Carya*	**Sycamore** *Platanus*
Beech *Fagus*	**Madrone** *Arbutus*	**Tupelo** *Nyssa*
Birch *Betula*	**Maple, Boxelder** *Acer*	**Walnut** *Juglans*
Cherry *Prunus*	**Mountain Ash, Dogberry, Rowan** *Sorbus*	**Willow** *Salix*
Crabapple *Malus*	**Mulberry** *Morus*	

10 Alder

Alnus

The banquet offered by alders attracts a variety of birds throughout the year. These are extremely important trees for insects, providing vital nutrition for migrating and nesting birds. A great many small birds, including redpolls and siskins, also gravitate to alder catkins to eat the seeds. The catkins attract insects, which, in turn, attract many tiny insectivorous birds, such as kinglets and warblers.

Alders are also very popular with sapsuckers, which drill the trees for sap; those sap wells, in turn, provide nutrition for Cape May Warblers and a host of insectivores who feed on minute insects also drawn to the sap. Woodpeckers, from the tiny Downy and Nuttall's to the enormous Pileated, often drill nest holes and roost holes in alders.

These are early successional trees, among the first to appear after disturbances near streams, rivers, and wetlands. Most thrive only near water.

USES
- Ornamental
- Soil improvement in wet areas

EXPOSURE: Sun, part shade, shade

SOIL MOISTURE: Moist

MOST USEFUL SEASON(S): Spring through fall

COLOR(S): Yellowish or greenish flowers and foliage

MAXIMUM HEIGHT: 80 feet (24 m)

NATIVE RANGE

Alders have a symbiotic relationship with a species of bacteria, *Frankia alni*, found in their root nodules. Sugars produced by the tree via photosynthesis feed the bacteria, which absorb nitrogen from the air, making it available to the tree. This allows alders to thrive even in poor soil. Ultimately this process improves the fertility of the soil, making the habitat better even as the short-lived alders die and are replaced by later successional trees.

YELLOW-BELLIED SAPSUCKER

RECOMMENDED SPECIES

Plant alders only in wet or moist areas. The Arizona alder (*Alnus oblongifolia*) is an important tree for birds in the sky islands of southeastern Arizona and southwestern New Mexico. Smooth alder (*A. serrulata*) is an eastern species, native from southern New England down through the eastern and south-central states. Gray or speckled alder (*A. incana*) is found in many of the northern states and provinces and in Southwestern mountains. White alder (*A. rhombifolia*) is found more patchily through California, Oregon, and Washington to western Idaho. Red alder (*A. rubra*) is found along the Pacific slope to the West Coast, from southern Alaska through central California.

During spring migration, Cape May Warblers are drawn to sapsucker drill holes.

11 Aspen, Cottonwood

Populus

HOST FOR SPONGY MOTHS; ROOTS SPREAD

Popular with humans for their bright yellow fall color, *Populus*, including aspens and cottonwood, are even more popular with birds, and for far more substantive reasons. Redpolls and siskins are especially fond of the seeds. In winter, the buds are an important food source for quail and grouse. Even prairie chickens, which normally shun trees, gravitate to these species when snow is deep.

Fungal growth causes a condition called heart rot in many kinds of trees. The inside of an aspen can be rotted sawdust even as the outer wood looks perfectly healthy.

PRAIRIE CHICKENS

Bracket fungi growing on a trunk is a good indication that the wood is slowly decaying from the inside as well.

Populus trees have very soft wood, so are especially prone to heart rot, making them a preferred nesting tree for Pileated Woodpeckers. They use their long, chiseled beak to hack the hole we see through healthy wood, and then reach in and scoop out the soft decayed wood from the heart of the tree to create a large nest chamber. Pileated Woodpeckers usually use a nest cavity for just one brood, after which small nesting owls or flying squirrels may take it over.

In the north, aspens are a favorite of native forest tent caterpillars, or "army worms." The moths lay their egg masses in summer on aspens, as well as on several other deciduous trees; the eggs overwinter and the larvae hatch in spring. These hairy caterpillars can have serious population explosions some springs, usually in cycles of about a decade. In

PILEATED WOODPECKERS

RUBY-CROWNED KINGLET

continued on next page

NATIVE RANGE

USES
- Ornamental
- Bright yellow fall colors

EXPOSURE: Sun

SOIL MOISTURE: Average

MOST USEFUL SEASON(S): Year-round

COLOR(S): Green, turning yellow in fall

MAXIMUM HEIGHT: 80 feet (24 m)

BLACK-BILLED CUCKOO

SPONGY MOTH

outbreak years, large stands of aspens can be entirely defoliated, though the trees grow new leaves that same year and seldom are injured by the caterpillars. During forest tent caterpillar outbreaks, Black-billed Cuckoo numbers also explode—this is one of the few birds adept at eating hairy caterpillars.

Unfortunately, aspens are also a favored host of a very destructive invasive exotic pest, the spongy moth.

RECOMMENDED SPECIES

For several reasons, *Populus* trees are seldom specifically planted for landscaping small backyards. They're almost like weeds, growing without our help in appropriate habitat. Many of them grow via root suckers, quickly sprouting into far more trees than homeowners may want. Their cottony seeds—especially those of cottonwoods—are released in such huge numbers that they can clog gutters and air-conditioner filters. And their spreading roots gravitate to water, sometimes damaging sewer and water pipes. But planted in the back of a medium-size or large yard, away from the house and underground pipes, they provide food and shelter for a great many birds.

Quaking aspen (*P. tremuloides*) is the state tree of Utah and the defining species of the "aspen parkland" habitat in the Prairie Provinces and northern Minnesota.

It is among the few trees with **photosynthetic** bark, allowing it to produce nutrients necessary for growth even after leaves have fallen in fall and winter. This nutritious bark also makes it a favorite for mammals to eat in winter. Perhaps because those mammals prefer to strip the bark on quaking aspen, bigtooth aspen (*P. grandidentata*) is a bit more disease-resistant; it can also tolerate drier conditions than can quaking aspen.

Eastern cottonwood (*P. deltoides*), the state tree of Kansas, Nebraska, and Wyoming, is an especially important host for several moths and butterflies, including mourning cloak, red-spotted purple, viceroy, and tiger swallowtail. It's also much more resistant than quaking aspen to deer browsing on its bark.

Talk to local gardeners about which are the best choices for your location, not only to help birds but also to learn what problems they might pose in your backyard setting.

Close Connection

In spring, *Populus* trees are vital to early migrants, the catkins and emerging leaves providing tiny insect food for such insectivores as hummingbirds, kinglets, and warblers. The sap is a favorite of sapsuckers, which drill holes that also attract many other birds, especially Ruby-throated Hummingbirds and Cape May Warblers in the East. Both species feed on the running sap as well as insects attracted to sapsucker drill holes.

The northward spring progression of Ruby-throated Hummingbirds is conveniently timed so that the tiny birds arrive a couple of weeks after Yellow-bellied Sapsuckers do, ensuring the hummers have plenty of food before many flowers have opened.

A Ruby-throated Hummingbird sips from sapsucker holes.

12 Basswood

Tilia

American basswood is an important component of eastern deciduous climax forests. Many birds, from chickadees to Wood Ducks, nest in natural cavities formed when basswood limbs break off; woodpeckers excavate other cavities that they and then other birds use. Sapsuckers are drawn to basswood, followed by many other birds that feed on the fluid and insects in the sapsuckers' drill holes.

Bees, a great many other insects, and sometimes Ruby-throated Hummingbirds are drawn to the nectar-rich flowers. Those flowers also attract many insectivores. With the loss of

BLACK-THROATED
BLUE WARBLER

USES
- Reforestation
- Shade tree
- Ornamental

EXPOSURE: Sun to shade

SOIL MOISTURE: Average

MOST USEFUL SEASON(S): Year-round

COLOR(S): Flowers white

MAXIMUM HEIGHT: 80 feet (24 m)

NATIVE RANGE

elm trees, American basswood has become a good nesting alternative for Baltimore Orioles. In northern Minnesota, Black-throated Blue Warblers are most reliably found in maple-basswood forests.

Basswood grows much faster than many other large trees, often starting to flower and produce seeds for the first time barely a decade after sprouting. Mature trees produce heavy shade. Basswood is often planted on the windward side of an orchard to protect young and delicate trees.

RECOMMENDED SPECIES
Our native basswood is American basswood (*Tilia americana*). The European littleleaf linden (*T. cordata*) is often grown as a shade tree, but European basswood species are implicated in some rare poisonings of bumble bees.

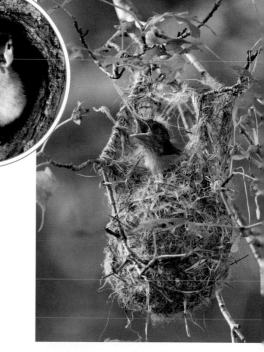

Left: Wood Ducks peer from their nest in a basswood cavity. **Right:** With the loss of elm trees, Baltimore Orioles often now choose to nest in basswoods.

GREAT CRESTED FLYCATCHER

13

Beech

Fagus

When large swaths of forest are allowed to reach their climax stage of succession, in most of eastern North America, the two most prevalent trees are beech and maple. The importance of American beech for birds can't be overstated.

Tufted Titmice and Wood Thrushes are among the huge variety of eastern birds that thrive in beech-maple forests. Wood Thrushes often incorporate the previous year's dead beech leaves into their nests. The natural cavities formed when beech branches fall, as well as those excavated by woodpeckers, provide important nesting and roosting for Barred Owls, Great Crested Flycatchers, and many other birds.

Beechnuts are an important food for birds from tiny Tufted Titmice to Wild Turkeys, and they were one of the primary foods of the now-extinct Passenger Pigeon. Market hunting and indiscriminate shooting of huge flocks of Passenger Pigeons passing through settled areas were the final cause of the species' extinction. The eastern beech-maple forest fragmented as cities and farms sprang up, making the pigeons more vulnerable in the first place.

It takes about four decades for beech trees to mature and six decades before large crops of beech-nut can be produced, but even young beeches provide nest sites and a smorgasbord of food for birds, from high-protein insects to sap.

RECOMMENDED SPECIES

Our only native beech, the American beech (*Fagus grandifolia*) is one of the most shade-tolerant of all trees. It is a poor choice in urban settings and even many suburban backyards, however, because of its extensive root system (which can damage buildings) and its intolerance of air pollution, compacted soil, and salt. The fragile bark of American beech—the very feature that makes carving initials into it so historically popular—makes it vulnerable to a fungal infection called beech bark disease, usually transmitted via insect damage.

These issues explain why it can be very difficult to purchase American beech in local garden stores; North American landscapers usually plant European beech (*F. sylvatica*) because its many cultivars are easily grown in backyards. It's usually better, though, to choose a locally native tree of a different genus. If you want to plant American beech and can't find it locally, you may need to buy bare-root trees by mail.

BEECH

USES
- Ornamental
- Shade tree
- Edible nuts

EXPOSURE: Partial sun to shade

SOIL MOISTURE: Average

MOST USEFUL SEASON(S): Year-round

COLOR(S): Flowers yellow, green, brown; leaves copper-colored in fall, may cling to the tree well into winter

MAXIMUM HEIGHT: 80 feet (24 m)

NATIVE RANGE

14 Birch

Betula

Providing abundant food for insects, birches support a great many migrating and nesting birds. Redpolls and chickadees feed heavily on birch catkins, and grouse eat both the catkins and buds. Birches are very important feeding trees for sapsuckers and for the birds drawn to their sap wells (see box on page 66). Broad-winged Hawks often prefer them as nesting trees.

Birches are **pioneer species** that are part of early succession after wildfires, windstorms, or avalanches clear an area. Their lightweight, wind-borne seeds sprout on disturbed soil, often leading to single-species stands until later successional trees and other plants can work their way in.

BROAD-WINGED HAWK

USES
- Ornamental
- Shade tree
- Land reclamation
- Erosion control

EXPOSURE: Sun to partial shade

SOIL MOISTURE: Average to moist

MOST USEFUL SEASON(S): Year-round

COLOR(S): Paper birch bark is white; flowers and catkins greenish to brown; leaves green, turning yellow in fall

MAXIMUM HEIGHT: 75 feet (23 m)

NATIVE RANGE

Stands of birches are fairly fire resistant under normal conditions, but these trees can be extremely flammable during droughts. Never plant a birch near a black walnut—the walnut roots exude a chemical very toxic to birches.

RECOMMENDED SPECIES

Paper birch (*Betula papyrifera*), the provincial tree of Saskatchewan and state tree of New Hampshire, is the most popular birch as a landscape tree. In natural forests it usually has a single trunk, but in backyards it often develops multiple trunks. Although birch roots are shallow, high winds tend to break them at the trunk rather than uproot them.

In the southern parts of its natural range this species can be very short lived, barely living three or four decades, but in the far north it can survive a century or more. Its leaves need as much sun as possible, but like most birches it needs cool, moist soil for its wide, shallow root system, so planting it on the north or west side of a house is preferable to a southern or eastern exposure.

Ruffed Grouse feed heavily on birch catkins in winter.

continued on next page

Sap Wells

Birches are essential feeding trees for sapsuckers, who dig tiny, shallow holes into the bark, often in straight rows around the trunk. The sap oozing out of these holes attracts not only birds that feed on the sweet fluid but also birds that feed on insects drawn to the "sap wells."

SAPSUCKER DRILL HOLES

Yellow birch (*B. alleghaniensis*), the provincial tree of Quebec, is North America's largest birch and the most important for lumber. Its seeds cannot penetrate leaf litter, so they usually germinate on mossy, decaying logs. As yellow birches grow older, their "nurse logs" eventually rot away, sometimes leaving the birch standing atop stilt-like roots. Yellow birch saplings cannot establish in full shade, so like other birches they usually take root after a disturbance.

Sweet birch (*B. lenta*), belying its name, is not very palatable for deer, while yellow birch is heavily browsed. Where deer are abundant, sweet birch thickets may protect more vulnerable trees and other plants. Unfortunately, this species is harder to find in nurseries than most native birches.

River birch (*B. nigra*) is the most heat-tolerant of all the birches. As its name implies, it's generally associated with floodplains and swamps, but in the Southeast it's often planted for land reclamation and erosion control following mining operations.

Even though they're short lived in many backyards, birch trees provide food for birds such as woodpeckers and chickadees long after they topple.

BLACK-CAPPED CHICKADEE

NUTTALL'S WOODPECKER

15 Cherry

Prunus

Belonging to the genus *Prunus*, cherries are extremely valuable for birds. At least 429 species of native caterpillars have been documented on cherry trees, providing high-quality protein for a great many birds. Waxwings often eat the blossoms; the fruits provide excellent nutrition for these and many, many other birds. A variety of small birds nest in the branches or in cavities in the trunk and larger limbs.

Cherries are fairly short lived, but if left standing for a few years after they die, they provide nesting opportunities for woodpeckers, chickadees, nuthatches, and wrens.

continued on next page

NATIVE RANGE

USES
- Ornamental
- Small landscaping tree
- Edible fruits

EXPOSURE: Full sun to partial shade

SOIL MOISTURE: Average

MOST USEFUL SEASON(S): Spring through fall

COLOR(S): Foliage green; blossoms white, pink; fruits red

MAXIMUM HEIGHT: 80 feet (24 m); most much smaller

RECOMMENDED SPECIES

Pin cherries (*Prunus pensylvanica*) grow quickly but live only a few decades. Their seeds can remain dormant in the soil for many years after the parent tree has died, often sprouting after a fire to capitalize on the nutrients in the ash.

BLACK CHERRY

CHOKECHERRY

Black cherries (*P. serotina*) and chokecherry (*P. virginiana*) are closely related; the chokecherry is more shrublike. Both species are valuable for birds, but orchard owners dislike them because they're a natural host for tent caterpillars, which also attack cultivated fruit trees. Hollyleaf cherry (*P. ilicifolia*) is native to coastal California and desert chaparral areas of the Mojave Desert.

Gardeners and cooks tend to think of just two kinds of cherries: sweet cherries, which are various cultivars of *P. avium* (literally "bird cherry"); and sour cherries, which are cultivars of *P. cerasus*. The two wild species are native to Europe and western Asia. North American birds love to eat

Left: This cavity, originally constructed by Downy Woodpeckers for their nest, was successfully used the next year by Black-capped Chickadees to produce these chicks. Right: Mourning Doves sometimes nest in cherry, plum, and other fruit trees.

domesticated cherry varieties as much as we humans do, to the consternation of orchard growers. These cultivated varieties are not particularly invasive, so there are few caveats about planting cherries for human consumption, but native species are a better choice if you're planting for birds and other wildlife.

Native wild plums (*P. americana*) and their domesticated cultivars grow as trees or shrubs. The Canada or black plum (*P. nigra*) is probably the one referred to in the title of Laura Ingalls Wilder's book, *On the Banks of Plum Creek*, set near Walnut Grove, Minnesota. Mexican plum (*P. mexicana*) is found in the central states, eastern Texas, and down into Mexico.

WILD PLUMS

ROBIN FAMILY IN CRABAPPLE

16 Crabapple

Malus

Apple blossoms appeal to birds as well as to humans. Cedar Waxwings eat the petals; hummingbirds feed on the nectar. And a great many birds devour the insects that are also attracted to those flowers.

As leaves emerge, many other insects hatch on apple trees, providing plenty of protein for birds in spring and summer. The branches provide nest sites for some, including hummingbirds, and as trees get old, chickadees and small woodpeckers often excavate nest cavities in the trunk or in sturdy older branches. Sapsuckers tend to work on crabapples in autumn.

Some birds feed on crabapples when they first turn red, but plenty of apples can remain on the tree through winter, becoming softer and sweeter and providing an important food source for wintering fruit-eaters as other berries and fruits are depleted.

USES
- Ornamental
- Edible fruits

EXPOSURE: Sun to partial sun

SOIL MOISTURE: Average, well drained

MOST USEFUL SEASON(S): Year-round

COLOR(S): Blossoms pink to white

MAXIMUM HEIGHT: 30 feet (9 m)

NATIVE RANGE

RECOMMENDED SPECIES

Locally native crabapples should be fairly easy to find. Some good choices are sweet crabapple (*Malus coronaria*), Oregon crabapple (*M. fusca*), southern crabapple (*M. angustifolia*), and prairie and Texas crabapple (natural variants of *M. ioensis*).

Some people eat native crabapples, but most apples grown for human consumption are cultivars of *M. domestica*—a panoply of hybrids and selectively grown varieties that originated with the wild apple (*M. sieversii*) of central Asia. These domesticated cultivars aren't particularly invasive and do benefit birds, especially bluebirds, which gravitate to apple orchards for nesting and feeding. But if you're planting trees specifically to benefit birds, native species are a better choice.

DOWNY WOODPECKER

RUBY-THROATED HUMMINGBIRD

17 Desert Willow

Chilopsis

Growing as a tree or as a spreading shrub, desert willow has willowlike foliage but is in the catalpa family, unrelated to willows. Its flowers attract hummingbirds and its seeds feed a variety of birds, including White-winged Doves. Ladder-backed Woodpeckers excavate nest cavities in it, Ash-throated Flycatchers occasionally nest in the split trunk, and doves and Verdins nest in the branches.

WHITE-WINGED DOVE

VERDIN

USES
- Ornamental

EXPOSURE: Sun

SOIL MOISTURE: Dry to moist; drought tolerant

MOST USEFUL SEASON(S): Flowers appear after summer rains; seed pods remain well into fall

COLOR(S): Flowers showy pink, white

MAXIMUM HEIGHT: 35 feet (11 m)

NATIVE RANGE

RECOMMENDED SPECIES

Desert willow (*Chilopsis linearis*) is the only species in this genus. Its natural growth is irregular, but it can be pruned into a conventional tree or shrub shape. It blooms best for the longest period if allowed to dry completely between waterings; excessive water and fertilizer result in a weaker, more spindly plant that doesn't bloom well. Native desert plants like this one virtually never need watering.

Left: Ladder-backed Woodpeckers often excavate nest cavities in desert willow. **Right:** Greater Roadrunners don't spend all their time on the ground. This one is perched in desert willow.

18 Hackberry

Celtis

Often called sugarberries, hackberries are very popular landscape trees—handsome, drought tolerant, and bearing nectar-rich flowers and attractive berries. They supply migrating and nesting birds with abundant insects, and robins, waxwings, mockingbirds, and a great many other birds feed on their sweet fruits.

Verdin and White-winged Doves nest within desert hackberry, the only plant in the genus with thorns. Hackberries are often parasitized by mistletoe, which slowly kills the tree but also feeds a lot of birds.

A Northern Mockingbird feeds on desert hackberry.

USES
- Ornamental
- Fencerows

EXPOSURE: Part shade

SOIL MOISTURE: Medium

MOST USEFUL SEASON(S): Year-round

COLOR(S): Foliage and flowers green; fruits orange-red to black

MAXIMUM HEIGHT: 100 feet (30 m)

NATIVE RANGE

RECOMMENDED SPECIES

The leaves of some species, especially southern hackberry or sugarberry (*Celtis laevigata*), contain chemicals that inhibit seed germination and growth of other plants. Southern hackberry reaches its northern extreme in Missouri and Illinois, east to the Carolinas down to Florida and west to Oklahoma and Texas.

Common hackberry (*C. occidentalis*) is a good choice in the central and east-central states, as is western hackberry (*C. reticulata*) in its patchier range from Washington and Oregon south to California and east to Nebraska, Oklahoma, and Texas. Desert or spiny hackberry (*C. ehrenbergiana*) ranges from the southwestern third of Texas through southwest New Mexico and southeast Arizona.

White-winged Doves nest in desert hackberry.

19 Hickory, Pecan

Carya

Favored host plants for beautiful moths, including the stunning luna moth, hickories and pecans are native in the eastern United States and Canada (pecans grown in Florida and California are not locally native). Many species are rare and declining.

A great many birds, including ducks, Northern Bobwhite, and Wild Turkeys, feed on the seeds and nuts; smaller birds feed on the catkins as well as the seeds; and many insectivorous birds are drawn to larvae that hickories host. Sapsuckers drill into some hickories for sap, sometimes causing the bark to get streaked. Many birds also nest in hickories.

RECOMMENDED SPECIES

Twelve species of hickory, including pecan, are native to eastern North America. Shagbark hickory (*Carya ovata*) is fairly widespread, found throughout most of the eastern states and barely into southeastern

USES
- Ornamental
- Edible nuts

EXPOSURE: Sun, part shade, shade

SOIL MOISTURE: Average

MOST USEFUL SEASON(S): Spring through fall

COLOR(S): Flowers green to brown; leaves golden in fall

MAXIMUM HEIGHT: 120 feet (37 m)

NATIVE RANGE

Canada, but not along the Atlantic and Gulf coastal plains or lower Mississippi Delta. The range of the pignut hickory (*C. glabra*) doesn't extend as far west as that of shagbark hickory but does include the Atlantic and Gulf coastal plains and reaches into the northern third of Florida.

Shellbark hickory (*C. laciniosa*) is rare and declining, listed as Endangered in Maryland and Threatened in New York. It's slow growing and difficult to transplant, but within its range on loam soils is worth nurturing. The even rarer and more localized nutmeg hickory (*C. myristiciformis*) is also worth nurturing.

Black hickory (*C. texana*) is listed as Endangered in Indiana—this rare species, endemic to the United States, is found only in the southern Great Plains and the lower Mississippi Valley. The scrub hickory (*C. floridana*) is endemic to central Florida, where it is an important component of scrub habitat.

Screech-Owls and other cavity nesters take advantage of the natural cavities that form in these trees.

WILD TURKEYS

PAINTED BUNTING

CEDAR WAXWING

20 Madrone

Arbutus

Handsome evergreen broadleaf trees, madrones have glossy leaves, large clusters of small white flowers that produce orange-red fruits, and showy, reddish, peeling bark. Hummingbirds are drawn to the flowers.

Many birds, including quail, Band-tailed Pigeons and other doves, American Robins, Varied Thrushes, and Cedar Waxwings, feed on the fruits, and a great many more on the insects madrones host. In a mixed stand, madrones are selected more often than are neighboring trees by nest-building birds.

Pacific madrone depends on intermittent natural fires to reduce conifer numbers; mature madrones can survive most natural fires, and large numbers of madrone seeds sprout following fires. Tragically, recent fires, exacerbated by high temperatures and extreme drought conditions, are taking a toll even on this fire-tolerant tree.

USES
- Reforestation
- Shade garden
- Ornamental

EXPOSURE: Sun to part shade

SOIL MOISTURE: Dry to moist

MOST USEFUL SEASON(S): Year-round

COLOR(S): Flowers white

MAXIMUM HEIGHT: 100 feet (30 m)

NATIVE RANGE

The Soberanes Fire in 2016, caused by an illegal campfire, severely burned the largest known specimen, located in the Joshua Creek Canyon Ecological Reserve on the Big Sur Coast. That tree was listed in the American Forests National Register of Champion Trees.

RECOMMENDED SPECIES

Pacific madrone (*Arbutus menziesii*) is found in coastal forests from Vancouver Island, British Columbia to Santa Barbara, California. It's declining throughout its range. It's extremely sensitive to changes in the grade or drainage near the root crown, so development has taken a serious toll. Rising temperatures and more frequent droughts are almost certainly part of the problem, too.

Arizona madrone (*A. arizonica*) is found in the sky islands of southeastern Arizona and southwestern New Mexico, and well into Mexico. Texas madrone (*A. xalapensis*) is found in the Edwards Plateau and the Trans-Pecos area of Texas into New Mexico and throughout Mexico.

STRAWBERRY ARBUTUS

ANNA'S HUMMINGBIRD

RED MAPLE

21 Maple, Boxelder

Acer

The maple leaf on the Canadian flag is ample proof of this tree's importance and popularity with humans. Maples are one of the most dominant species in eastern North America's climax forests. They host hundreds of species of native caterpillars that feed migrating and nesting birds. Their winged seeds—called samaras and given such nicknames as helicopters, whirlybirds, and maple keys—are an essential food source for many birds, especially Evening Grosbeaks.

This Evening Grosbeak is feeding on boxelder samaras.

BOXELDER

SUGAR MAPLE

continued on next page

MAPLE, BOXELDER **81**

NATIVE RANGE

USES
- Shade tree
- Shelterbelts
- Ornamental
- Fall color

EXPOSURE: Sun to shade

SOIL MOISTURE: Average

MOST USEFUL SEASON(S): Spring insects; summer and autumn seeds; fall color

COLOR(S): Foliage spectacular orange or red in fall

MAXIMUM HEIGHT: 150 feet (46 m)

Many songbirds nest in maple branches. White-breasted Nuthatches frequently nest in maple cavities, as do many woodpeckers. Large woodpecker holes and naturally formed cavities also provide nesting and roosting for owls.

Some maple species, such as boxelder and red maple, are very fast growing; others, such as sugar maple, grow much more slowly but live longer.

RECOMMENDED SPECIES

EASTERN SCREECH-OWL

RUBY-THROATED HUMMINGBIRD

The sugar maple (*Acer saccharum*) is the state tree of New York, Vermont, West Virginia, and Wisconsin. Sugar maples don't reach seed-bearing age for about three decades, but in northern forests they typically live for 200 years and some even reach the three-century mark. Even when too young to produce seeds, they're furnishing a rich supply of insect food for birds. Sugar maple is very sensitive to air pollution, acid rain, and road salt; that's why it's been displaced in many cities and towns by Norway maple (*A. platanoides*), a nonnative.

Sugar maple seeds must undergo a hard freeze for proper dormancy and only germinate when temperatures are slightly above freezing, so climate change is shifting the sugar maple's range northward. Collection of sap for sugar isn't possible where winter temperatures aren't cold enough.

Red maple (*A. rubrum*), the state tree of Rhode Island, is one of the most abundant and widespread native trees in eastern North America. It's very fast growing in a wide range of soil types and climate conditions. More abundant now than when Europeans first arrived in North America, red maple thrives in areas after disturbances. Red maple and its close relative the silver maple (*A. saccharinum*) are the only maples that produce their seeds in spring rather than fall.

Bigtooth maple (*A. grandidentatum*) is an excellent choice where it's native, from southeast Idaho south to Arizona and east to southern New Mexico and western Texas, and locally in southwest Oklahoma and the Edwards Plateau of south-central Texas.

Boxelder (*A. negundo*) is very widespread, and in the East is often considered a "weed tree." It's hardy and fast growing, but easily broken in storms and relatively short lived. When the seeds are not all consumed by birds and squirrels, they often remain on trees into winter, sometimes serving as a conspicuous invitation to Evening Grosbeaks. Unlike other maples, boxelder trees are either male or female, so both are necessary for the females to produce seeds.

Top: These Red-bellied Woodpeckers successfully raised young in this boxelder. **Bottom:** A White-breasted Nuthatch feeds a fledgling in a boxelder.

22 Mountain Ash, Dogberry, Rowan

Sorbus

Sapsuckers often drill mountain ashes for sap, which benefits not just the sapsuckers but the many birds that then come to the drill holes for sap and attendant insects. The berries don't normally ripen until October, making them a valuable food source for late-migrating and wintering birds such as Ruffed, Dusky, Sooty, and Sharp-tailed Grouse, ptarmigans, jays, robins and other thrushes, and waxwings.

The fairly small size of mountain ash trees, the beauty of their flowers and berry clusters, and their exceptional cold tolerance make them excellent choices in many northern backyards. They tend to be short lived.

USES
- Ornamental

EXPOSURE: Sun, part sun, shade

SOIL MOISTURE: Average

MOST USEFUL SEASON(S): Spring into winter

COLOR(S): Foliage green; flowers white; berries orange-red

MAXIMUM HEIGHT: 30 feet (9 m)

NATIVE RANGE

RECOMMENDED SPECIES

Just about anywhere in the northern half of the continent except in the Great Plains, and south into Georgia's mountains, there may be a native mountain ash. Excellent choices in the East are the American mountain ash (*Sorbus americana*) and the even more winter-hardy showy mountain ash (*S. decora*). In the West, the choices include Greene's mountain ash (*S. scopulina*) and Sitka mountain ash (*S. sitchensis*).

Mountain ashes all prefer cool, moist areas, so planting them outside their native range or at lower elevations in central and southern states seldom works. There is no reason to plant European mountain ash to foster North American birds.

It's best to plant fruit trees that are extremely popular with birds, including mountain ash, well away from busy roads or windows, to minimize collisions.

YELLOW-BELLIED SAPSUCKER

CEDAR WAXWINGS

23 Mulberry

Morus

NONNATIVE SPECIES VERY INVASIVE

These small trees provide a wealth of fruits in spring and early summer for large numbers of birds. Many of those fruits fall to the ground and make a mess, but that's a small price to pay for those of us who love birds. Our native mulberries also provide a feast for insectivorous birds, and some birds nest within the foliage. People monitoring bird activity at a single mulberry tree in Arkansas recorded 31 different bird species!

RECOMMENDED SPECIES

North America has two native mulberry species. Red mulberry (*Morus rubra*) is the more widespread but is limited to the eastern half of the United States south of the northern border states. Texas mulberry (*M. microphylla*) is restricted to extreme southwestern Oklahoma, the western two-thirds of Texas, and the southern halves of New Mexico and Arizona. In these desert habitats the mulberry's moist fruits are especially valuable for birds.

USES
- Ornamental
- Edible fruits

EXPOSURE: Sun, part shade, shade

SOIL MOISTURE: Dry to moist

MOST USEFUL SEASON(S): Spring through fall

COLOR(S): Flowers white, green, brown; fruits red, purple, black

MAXIMUM HEIGHT: 36 feet (11 m)

NATIVE RANGE

An Asian species, white mulberry (*M. alba*), is very invasive. It's more cold-tolerant than our native red mulberry, and the two species hybridize. The hybrids can genetically overwhelm red mulberry, contributing to the endangered status of our native species at the northern edge of its range. You can identify invasive white mulberry by its smooth, shiny leaves; native red mulberry leaves are more sandpapery, with noticeable hairs on the upper surface. Conscientious landscapers should not just avoid planting white mulberry but also actively remove it. Unfortunately, white mulberry is still sold in many nurseries.

SCARLET TANAGER

FLORIDA SCRUB OAK

24

Oak

Quercus

From tiny acorns do mighty Wood Ducks, Wild Turkeys, Blue Jays, Florida Scrub-Jays, American Crows (and a wide variety of other animals, as well as new oaks) grow. Indeed, so many animals eat and squirrel away acorns that it's been estimated that only one in 10,000 acorns results in an eventual tree.

Mature oaks drop varying numbers of acorns every year. Every 4 to 10 years, some oak populations synchronize to produce almost no acorns at all, then drop huge numbers the following year, which is called a "mast year." Scientists believe that the years with virtually no acorns may reduce local acorn-dependent mammal populations, so that more acorns can survive to germinate during the next year's overproduction.

The benefits oaks provide to birds go far beyond bountiful acorns. Even small oak saplings provide vital food for migrating songbirds in the form of the many native caterpillars that hatch and grow in buds and emerging leaves.

Decades before they start producing flowers and acorns, oaks are critically important.

Many birds nest in oaks starting when leafy young branches provide enough cover; mature oaks supply nesting cavities as well. Even after death, standing oak snags provide nesting opportunities for such large species as herons and some hawks, as well as continued nesting and roosting opportunities for cavity-nesters.

Many oaks are pioneer species, germinating and growing after fire and other natural disasters clear an area. In areas where fires historically occurred with some regularity, many wildlife species have grown dependent on fire to keep providing new pioneer plants. For these animals, including Black-capped Vireos, Florida Scrub-Jays, and many others, fire suppression has reduced the amount of habitat they can use. Controlled burns or painstakingly removing the plants that grow at later successional stages and planting oaks can be essential for these birds to survive.

continued on next page

Close Connection

Blue Jays cache acorns in nooks and crannies well above ground, but they also "plant" a great many of them by storing them in the soil. They often cover a spot where they've hidden an acorn with a leaf. This helps the jay find it later and also keeps the soil a bit moister and cooler, improving the chances that the acorn will germinate if the jay doesn't return.

BLUE JAY

OAK

USES
- Ornamental
- Shade tree
- Edible acorns

EXPOSURE: Sun

SOIL MOISTURE: Dry to moist

MOST USEFUL SEASON(S): Year-round

COLOR(S): Foliage green, changing to yellow, orange, or brown in fall; flowers green

MAXIMUM HEIGHT: 100+ feet (30+ m) or even more

NATIVE RANGE

RECOMMENDED SPECIES

Oak trees are perhaps the single most important genus of deciduous trees for wildlife. Because most oaks have large tap roots, however, they aren't a good choice near buildings, on small lawns, or along sidewalks or streets.

Oaks belonging to three different taxonomic groups—"white," "red," and "intermediate"—are native to North America. Those in the "white oak" category produce acorns that mature in 6 months; the acorns can be sweet or only slightly bitter. Acorns of "red oaks" and "intermediate oaks" mature in 18 months and may be too bitter for some animals (humans may treat them to leach out the bitter-tasting tannins), but they are eaten by many birds. The species usually called simply the white oak (*Quercus alba*) has such long lower branches that it's not unusual for a white oak in an open area to be as wide as it is tall. It's closely related to both swamp white oak (*Q. bicolor*), which grows in moist and wet areas, and bur oak (*Q. macrocarpa*).

Bur oak, which has the largest acorns of any North American oak, is also one of the slowest growing, sometimes living over 300 years.

SAY'S PHOEBES

ANNA'S HUMMINGBIRDS

Bur oak is a very important tree in grasslands. Its thick bark makes it fairly fire tolerant, and a large taproot gives it protection against drought. The acorns of all three of these species are far less bitter than acorns of red or intermediate oaks and are eaten by a huge variety of birds and mammals.

BUR OAK ACORN

Scrub or shrub oaks such as Gambel oak (*Q. gambelii*) and California scrub oak (*Q. berberidifolia*) include several species that are all fairly short but not necessarily closely related; they, too, can belong to all three oak categories. The word *chaparral* comes from the Spanish word *chaparro*, which refers to scrub oak.

California black oaks (*Q. kelloggii*), which belong to the "red oak" category, occupy more total area in California than any other hardwood tree and are incredibly important for birds. In one study, all 68 bird species observed in oak woodlands in the Tehachapi Mountains foraged in California black oak at least part of the time, eating the abundant insects, berries on the mistletoe that often grows on this oak, and of course the acorns when available.

The "intermediate oak" category includes just a few species, such as the canyon live oak (*Q. chrysolepis*) and huckleberry oak (*Q. vacciniifolia*), all of the Southwest.

In 2004, the United States Congress designated the oak America's national tree. The generic oak is also the state tree of Iowa. The white oak is the state tree of Connecticut, Illinois, and Maryland. The northern red oak is the state tree of New Jersey and the provincial tree of Prince Edward Island.

Live Oaks

Various oaks that hold onto their leaves through the winter are called "live oaks." They don't keep the leaves forever—new leaves form every spring, the old leaves dropping just before new ones emerge.

Live oaks can belong to any of the three native oak groups. The iconic southern live oak (*Quercus virginiana*), the state tree of Georgia, is in the white oak category, as is the sand live oak (*Q. geminata*), which the rare and declining Florida Scrub-Jay prefers for nesting to any other tree. The interior live oak (*Q. wislizeni*) is a red oak.

25

Redbud
Cercis

A beautiful small tree or large shrub, redbud is the state tree of Oklahoma and a host to many caterpillars. It blooms early, drawing some beautiful migrants such as Rose-breasted Grosbeaks and Baltimore Orioles to its abundant insect food. It also provides nectar for hummingbirds, and its seeds feed many birds as well.

RECOMMENDED SPECIES

Eastern redbud (*Cercis canadensis*) has a fairly wide range in the eastern states; western redbud (*C. occidentalis*) is far more limited in range, from northern California east to southern Utah and southern Arizona, in canyons and slopes of foothills and mountains. Western redbud is common in Grand Canyon National Park.

NATIVE RANGE

USES
- Hedgerow
- Reforestation
- Shade garden
- Ornamental

EXPOSURE: Sun to shade

SOIL MOISTURE: Average

MOST USEFUL SEASON(S): Early spring into summer

COLOR(S): Flowers magenta

MAXIMUM HEIGHT: 30 feet (9 m)

26 Sycamore

Platanus

Migrating and nesting birds can find ample insect food in native North American sycamores. Woodpeckers often excavate nesting cavities in sycamore trunks; those cavities and the ones that form when branches fall provide nesting for Wood Ducks and Barred Owls. Great Crested, Dusky-capped, and Brown-crested Flycatchers are often found in sycamores, nesting in cavities, perching in branches, or sallying forth to catch flying insects.

Hummingbirds catch minute insects in the flowers, and they also use the downy blossoms as nesting material. Acorn Woodpeckers often use sycamores as their granaries, chiseling hundreds of tiny holes in which to stash their acorns. Many birds feed on sycamore seeds.

Sycamores have more massive trunks than any other North American hardwood trees, some over 10 feet (3 m) in diameter. Chimney Swifts once nested in the hollow trunks of old, giant sycamores.

continued on next page

WHISKERED SCREECH-OWL

GREAT BLUE HERON

In some sycamores, insect pests and mistletoe can cause "witches' brooms"—a deformity in which a dense mass of shoots grows from a single damaged point, with the resulting structure resembling a broom or a large bird's nest. These deformities remain on the tree for the remainder of its life but don't seem to hurt it. Flying squirrels (fun little mammals, even if they're not birds) often nest in witches' brooms.

RECOMMENDED SPECIES

Three species of sycamores are native to North America: the American sycamore (*Platanus occidentalis*) in the East, and the California sycamore (*P. racemosa*) and Arizona sycamore (*P. wrightii*) in the West. All are valuable and important trees within their ranges.

Trees in the genus *Platanus* are not related to what are called sycamores in the Old World—fig trees cultivated since ancient times. North American sycamores are related to what are called plane trees in the United Kingdom.

SYCAMORE

NATIVE RANGE

USES
- Large shade tree

EXPOSURE: Sun, part sun, shade

SOIL MOISTURE: Moist

MOST USEFUL SEASON(S): Year-round

COLOR(S): Flowers red, yellow, green, brown; round fruit brown

MAXIMUM HEIGHT: 100 feet (30 m)

27 Tupelo

Nyssa

Extremely popular among beekeepers in the Southeast, tupelo and black gum trees are also bird magnets. The nectar-rich flowers may not be right for hummingbirds but do attract bees and other insects. The variety of caterpillars these trees host brings in even more insectivores, such as warblers and vireos. Fruit-eating specialists such as robins, bluebirds, thrashers, catbirds, waxwings, and even woodpeckers feast on the berries.

GRAY CATBIRD

The furrowed bark is ideal for the beaks of foraging nuthatches and woodpeckers, and the trees are also favorites among cavity nesters such as Prothonotary Warblers. The leaves turn scarlet in fall, making this a very popular ornamental tree.

continued on next page

TUPELO

NATIVE RANGE

USES

- Reforestation
- Shade garden
- Ornamental

EXPOSURE: Sun

SOIL MOISTURE: Average to wet

MOST USEFUL SEASON(S): Year-round

COLOR(S): Flowers green; fall foliage scarlet

MAXIMUM HEIGHT: 50 feet (15 m)

RECOMMENDED SPECIES

In swampy areas and where soils are seasonally wet, water tupelo (*Nyssa aquatica*) and white tupelo (*N. ogeche*) are great choices. Black gum (*N. sylvatica*) is more widely distributed and adapted to drier soils.

WHITE-BREASTED NUTHATCH

PROTHONOTARY WARBLER

28

Walnut

Juglans

Large, rugged walnut trees are extremely popular with birds. The nuts of some *Juglans* species are too big for most songbirds to handle, but woodpeckers and jays can hack into them, and turkeys can swallow them whole, their gizzards grinding away the shell. Even tiny chickadees and titmice can peck a small hole in a walnut shell and then pick at bits of the nut within, or pick up pieces that squirrels and other rodents drop.

The nuts of other walnut species are easy for small birds to manage, and the trees host plenty of caterpillars for insectivorous birds to eat. A great many birds also nest in walnut foliage or cavities.

RECOMMENDED SPECIES

Walnuts are not a good choice if you have a small yard: Their roots, especially those of black walnut (*Juglans nigra*), produce a chemical toxic to many other plant roots, so should be planted at least 50 feet away from fruit trees or other vulnerable plants.

continued on next page

Six species of walnuts are native in North America, including the black walnut, and all six are declining throughout their range. Butternut or white walnut (*J. cinerea*) is listed as Threatened in Tennessee, Special Concern in Kentucky, and Exploitably Vulnerable in New York, and it's on Canada's endangered species list.

The northern California walnut (*J. hindsii*) is endemic to northern California. Little walnut (*J. microcarpa*), Arizona walnut (*J. major*), and California black walnut (*J. californica*) are our other native walnut species.

Top: Wild Turkeys can swallow even large walnuts whole. **Bottom:** Tufted Titmice relish any bits of walnuts they can access.

WALNUT

NATIVE RANGE

USES
- Shade tree
- Edible nuts

EXPOSURE: Sun, part shade

SOIL MOISTURE: Moist

MOST USEFUL SEASON(S): Spring through fall

COLOR(S): Flowers yellow, green, brown

MAXIMUM HEIGHT: 100 feet (30 m)

PEACHLEAF WILLOW

RUBY-CROWNED KINGLET

29 Willow

Salix

ROOTS AGGRESSIVE

North America is home to about a hundred different species of willows, and all of our native willow trees and shrubs are wonderful for birds. The fine-textured leaf litter under willows provides an excellent place for migrating and wintering thrushes, thrashers, sparrows, and other ground-feeders to search for food. Grouse and some other species feed on the buds in winter.

Among the very first plants to bud out in late winter and early spring, willows are a rich source of early insects. Mourning cloaks, the first butterflies to emerge in early spring, spend their larval stage in willows.

Aphids and other tiny insects cluster around willow buds and flowers, and caterpillars feed on the emerging leaves, turning willows into oases for the first hummingbirds, kinglets, warblers, and other tiny insectivores. Hummingbirds, Yellow Warblers, and other small birds line their nests with the soft, fine hairs on the seeds.

continued on next page

NATIVE RANGE

USES
- Ornamental
- Shade tree
- Erosion control
- Hedgerow
- Wetland restoration

EXPOSURE: Sun, part shade, shade

SOIL MOISTURE: Moist or wet

MOST USEFUL SEASON(S): Year-round, especially late winter/early spring

COLOR(S): Flowers white, green, brown

MAXIMUM HEIGHT: 100 feet (30 m)

Many songbirds, such as Yellow Warblers, weave fine fibers, including the hairs on willow seeds, into their nests.

Every willow tree is either male or female, so to get the willow seeds that are so valuable as food and nesting fibers, you must have both a male plant to produce pollen and a female to produce seeds. Willow roots seek out water very aggressively and can clog septic systems, storm drains, and sewer systems (especially older ones), so plant them well away from any of these on your (or your neighbor's) property.

These plants tend to be both fast growing and short lived, susceptible to damage from insects, disease, and wind. Many willows also sucker and spread, naturally replacing those that have died while forming dense thickets. You may have to spend a lot of time and energy cutting them back to prevent them from taking over too large an area.

RECOMMENDED SPECIES

Our native pussy willow (*Salix discolor*) is an excellent choice if you want your garden to foster the first avian arrivals and migrants in spring, since it flowers long before other hummingbird flowers open. In the East, black willow (*S. nigra*) is a fine choice where there is

space. The coyote or narrowleaf willow (*S. exigua*) is the widest-ranging native tree willow. The arroyo willow (*S. lasiolepis*) is restricted to the West.

Pussy willow and the long-beaked willow (*S. bebbiana*) are two of the species called "diamond willows," developing diamond-shaped cankers in response to a fungus, which make them very popular for wood carvers and furniture makers.

Leaves and bark from willows have long been used medicinally, especially as pain relievers. The active extract salicin, which our bodies metabolize into salicylic acid (aspirin), was named for the Latin word for willows, *salix*.

Some pussy willows and the storied weeping willow are exotics, with much less value for our native insects and birds.

Left: The sitka willow's soft down carries its windborne seeds far from the tree, even as birds use some of the fluff for their nests.
Upper right: Mourning Cloak butterfly larvae feast on willow.
Lower right: Aphids swarm over willow buds and flowers.

GRASSES

An endless expanse of wild grasses, no trees to break the horizon, may appear to some to be a vast wasteland. Don't be deceived. Prairie and natural meadows may appear structurally simple but are rich in biodiversity. Although a few grass species dominate the community, in the same way a few tree species dominate each forest community, a plethora of other plants make up the healthy grassland, providing abundant food and safe shelter for grassland animals.

Bobolinks, larks, meadowlarks, longspurs, a wide variety of sparrows, prairie chickens, Upland Sandpipers, Northern Harriers, and Short-eared Owls are just some of the birds dependent on healthy grasslands.

Bluestem
Andropogon

Indiangrass
Sorghastrum

Little Bluestem
Schizachyrium

Sideoats Grama
Bouteloua

Spartina, Cordgrass
Spartina, sometimes called *Sporobolus*

Switchgrass, Panic Grass
Panicum

Vetch
Vicia

30 Bluestem

Andropogon

Native to a wide range of grassland ecosystems, bluestem is **mid-successional**. That means that after a fire or other disturbance occurs, and then after the pioneer plants set the stage, bluestem will thrive until more and more shrubs and trees convert the land to forest. Several skippers and the common wood nymph butterflies depend on it as their larval host; they in turn attract insectivores, including kingbirds and other flycatchers, as well as **granivorous** (grain-feeding) birds.

As a bunchgrass, bluestem's large clumps serve as shelter for nesting and roosting for grassland birds of all sizes, as well as shade and cover from predators. Many birds such as Sedge Wrens, Grasshopper and Henslow's Sparrows, and Western Meadowlarks use the clumps as preferred sites for nests. The dried grasses offer materials for birds nesting in trees and shrubs as well as ground nesters.

Juncos, sparrows, endangered prairie chickens, and other birds eat the seeds, especially in winter.

continued on next page

103

Left: Greater Prairie Chickens shelter in bluestem clumps and feed on the seeds in winter. **Upper right:** The badly declining Lesser Prairie Chicken depends on bluestem grasses for nesting, cover, and food. **Lower right:** Sedge Wrens often nest in bluestem clumps, and they feed on the abundant insects on bluestem.

RECOMMENDED SPECIES

Taxonomists have separated many grasses (even little bluestem) from bluestem's genus, *Andropogon*, but there are still about a dozen species of *Andropogon* grasses in the United States and Canada.

Big bluestem (*A. gerardii*), the state grass of Illinois and Missouri and the official prairie grass of Manitoba, is a major component of the North American tallgrass prairie, also growing in the understory of open longleaf pine communities. It grows to a height of 3 to 10 feet (1 to 3 m), depending on soil and moisture conditions. It's drought tolerant but intolerant of too much shade.

Pinewoods bluestem (*A. arctatus*), listed as Threatened in Florida, is even better adapted to pinewoods communities in Florida, Alabama, and North Carolina. Bushy bluestem (*A. glomeratus*) grows well in low, moist areas with poor drainage but needs full sunlight.

USES

- Erosion control
- Borders, mixed borders
- Hedgerow
- Pasture/rangeland
- Wetland gardens (some species)

EXPOSURE: Sun

SOIL MOISTURE: Dry to moist

MOST USEFUL SEASON(S): Year-round

COLOR(S): Green, bluish in summer; brown, often with white flower heads, in winter

MAXIMUM HEIGHT: 10 feet (3 m)

NATIVE RANGE

Some landowners who graze cattle or horses dislike broomsedge bluestem (*A. virginicus*), also called sage grass. It has low nutritional value for large mammals most of the year and crowds out the nonnative weeds that cows and horses prefer, especially on disturbed, already overgrazed soils. But broomsedge bluestem and sand bluestem (*A. hallii*) are part of the critical habitat for the dangerously declining Lesser Prairie Chicken.

In winter, bluestem is tall and dense, providing cover for birds and mammals, and the seeds provide food for many small birds.

31 Indiangrass

Sorghastrum

The official state grass of Oklahoma and South Carolina, Indiangrass is native in tallgrass prairies and in areas of longleaf pine, growing quickly after fires. It provides nesting sites and protective cover for prairie chickens, quail, doves, and grassland sparrows.

Indiangrass also offers abundant food for birds: seeds in fall and winter, and grasshoppers, caterpillars, and butterflies from spring through fall for insectivores. It can grow in thick stands in lowlands.

USES
- Meadow and prairie gardens
- Soil stabilization
- Ornamental

EXPOSURE: Sun, part shade, shade

SOIL MOISTURE: Can handle both drought and occasional flooding

MOST USEFUL SEASON(S): Year-round; prettiest in early fall

COLOR(S): Green; flowers brown, yellow

MAXIMUM HEIGHT: 8 feet (2.4 m); slow growth until late summer

NATIVE RANGE

RECOMMENDED SPECIES

Yellow Indiangrass (*Sorghastrum nutans*) is the most widespread species. Excellent choices in the plant's southeastern range are lopsided Indiangrass (*S. secundum*), found in the Atlantic and Gulf coastal plains and the southeastern mountains and Piedmont, and slender Indiangrass (*S. elliottii*), listed as Endangered in Maryland.

NORTHERN BOBWHITE

MOURNING DOVE

32 Little Bluestem

Schizachyrium

One of the most widespread of North America's native grasses, little bluestem provides insectivorous birds with grasshoppers and caterpillars as well as the moths and butterflies these become. Its seeds are an important food for sparrows and juncos, especially in winter. It also provides cover, nesting sites, and nesting materials for a wide variety of birds.

Since little bluestem is tough and adaptable, establishing quickly on disturbed soils, it can be used on banks and slopes and in restoration projects. Some species are valuable in sandy beach and dune habitats.

Little bluestem is the official state grass of Kansas and Nebraska.

USES

- Beach/prairie restoration/wildflower garden
- Meadows
- Ornamental

EXPOSURE: Full sun

SOIL MOISTURE: Well drained

MOST USEFUL SEASON(S): Year-round

COLOR(S): Flowers green, white, purple, brown

MAXIMUM HEIGHT: 1 to 5 feet (0.3 to 1.5 m)

NATIVE RANGE

RECOMMENDED SPECIES

The most widespread species is little bluestem (*Schizachyrium scoparium*). Gulf bluestem (*S. maritimum*), native to the Gulf Coast from Louisiana to the Florida Panhandle, is extremely important in coastal habitats. Dune bluestem (*S. littorale* or *S. scoparium* ssp. *littorale*) is a very important coastal plant found in sand dune habitat in the eastern and southern coastal strip of the United States and the shores of the Great Lakes. Texas bluestem (*S. cirratum*) grows on rocky slopes, usually at elevations of 5,000 feet (1524 m) and higher, in California, Arizona, New Mexico, and Texas.

Pinescrub bluestem (*S. niveum*) is found only in openings and sandhills of pine-oak woodlands in Florida, where it is listed as Endangered. Florida little bluestem (*S. rhizomatum*) is also restricted to Florida. Creeping little bluestem (*S. scoparium* ssp. *stoloniferum*) is found in Mississippi, Alabama, Florida, Georgia, and the Carolinas. It's the most widespread little bluestem in Florida.

DARK-EYED JUNCO

COMMON YELLOWTHROAT

33 Sideoats Grama

Bouteloua

Found only in the Americas, with most diversity in the Southwest, sideoats grama is one of the few native grasses that can be mowed and stands up to foot traffic. In general, *Bouteloua* supports grasshoppers and several butterfly larvae, especially skippers, providing vital food for insectivorous birds. Many birds eat the grasses' seeds, and some also use the grasses as nesting materials.

RECOMMENDED SPECIES

Sideoats grama (*Bouteloua curtipendula*) is the state grass of Texas. Blue grama (*B. gracilis*) is an important native grass throughout the Great Plains and the Southwest because of its drought resistance.

Buffalo grass (*B. dactyloides*) is an important drought-resistant native grass. Don't confuse it with buffelgrass (*Cenchrus ciliaris*), a noxious weed native to Africa and Asia that is causing serious habitat loss and fire damage in the American Southwest (see page 19).

American Robins use dried grama grasses in nest construction.

NATIVE RANGE

USES
- Wildflower meadows
- Prairie restoration
- Garden accents

EXPOSURE: Full sun, part shade, shade

SOIL MOISTURE: Moist to dry; drought tolerant

MOST USEFUL SEASON(S): Year-round where there is no snow

COLOR(S): Flowers green, purple, brown, white

MAXIMUM HEIGHT: 2 feet (0.6 m)

SKIPPER
BUTTERFLY

34 Spartina, Cordgrass

Spartina; sometimes called *Sporobolus*

Serving as pollution filters and buffers against flooding and shoreline erosion, native cordgrasses and other *Spartina* can be beneficial for coastal and prairie habitats, even tolerating some petroleum contamination. They support many crustaceans and mollusks, critical for coastal bird survival, and are essential hosts for several caterpillars, especially skippers, which in turn feed insectivorous birds.

Cordgrass seeds feed a variety of granivorous birds, and the plants provide nesting sites and cover for ducks, rails, and other coastal species, such as Seaside Sparrows. Geese and Sandhill Cranes spend a lot of time feeding and resting in cordgrass stands, the geese often grazing the tender shoots during the winter following early autumn burns. Mottled Ducks nest in dense clumps of cordgrass.

USES
- Beach restoration
- Erosion control

EXPOSURE: Sun

SOIL MOISTURE: Wet or moist

MOST USEFUL SEASON(S): Year-round

COLOR(S): Greens and browns

MAXIMUM HEIGHT: 7 feet (2 m)

NATIVE RANGE

Prairie cordgrass is found in many wet habitats, including wet prairies, floodplains, and marshes, and along ponds and rivers. Several moth caterpillars are dependent on this plant, and many other insects feed on it, all providing food for insectivorous birds. As with coastal cordgrasses, inland cordgrasses provide cover and nesting habitat.

RECOMMENDED SPECIES

On the East Coast and along the Gulf of Mexico, salt-meadow cordgrass or salt hay (*Spartina patens*) and smooth or saltmarsh cordgrass (*S. alterniflora*) are excellent choices for coastal properties. Inland, prairie cordgrass (*S. pectinata*) is the right choice.

California cordgrass (*S. foliosa*) is locally native in salt marshes and mudflats of coastal California, especially in San Francisco Bay. Unfortunately, both Eastern salt hay and dense-flowered cordgrass (*S. densiflora*) are invasive and destructive along the West Coast, crowding out California's native cordgrass as well as the endemic, endangered soft bird's beak (*Cordylanthus mollis*) and Pacific pickleweed (*Salicornia pacifica*). The only two *Spartina* species endemic to Oregon, Washington, and British Columbia are inland species, prairie cordgrass and *S. gracilis*.

Clapper Rails live in habitat dominated by saltmarsh cordgrass and salt hay.

The near-threatened Ridgway's Rail depends on California cordgrass and Pacific pickleweed, which are crowded out by invasive cordgrasses.

35 Switchgrass, Panic Grass

Panicum

**NONNATIVES
INVASIVE**

Many people are now familiar with switchgrass as a biofuel. When grown as a monoculture, it doesn't offer advantages for birds and other wildlife, especially when it's harvested during nesting season. But when mixed with other plants, it's a vital component of quality native grassland and field habitat, providing food for both insectivores and granivores plus excellent cover and nesting habitat. Upland game birds including doves, pheasants, quail, turkeys, and a variety of songbirds are drawn to open habitat that includes switchgrass.

RECOMMENDED SPECIES

Switchgrass (*Panicum virgatum*) is a widespread grass, most abundant in long-grass prairie habitat, but not native in Western coastal states or provinces, nor in Alberta or the Northwest Territories, where witchgrass

USES
- Prairie restoration
- Erosion control
- Ornamental

EXPOSURE: Sun, part shade

SOIL MOISTURE: Moist, dry

MOST USEFUL SEASON(S): Year-round

COLOR(S): Green to yellowish

MAXIMUM HEIGHT: 5 feet (1.5 m)

NATIVE RANGE

(*P. capillare*) is the native *Panicum* grass. Locally native Eastern panic grasses such as bitter panic grass (*P. amarum*) can serve as excellent beach grasses along the mid-Atlantic and Gulf coasts.

But the West Coast beach habitat is much more fragile. Both European beach grass (*Ammophila arenaria*) and American beach grass (*A. breviligulata*) have become invasive, making life tougher for the Snowy Plover, whose West Coast population is listed as Threatened. If you own or manage coastal property, work with knowledgeable native plant experts to find the best ways to protect your property and the birds who share it.

Left: The Pacific coast population of Snowy Plovers is listed as Threatened. These elegant little shorebirds nest on very sparsely vegetated beaches, and beachgrasses can grow too dense for them to nest. **Right:** Bobolinks, found in mixed grasslands, feed on *Panicum* seeds and the insects these grasses host.

36 Vetch

Vicia

NONNATIVES INVASIVE

A legume commonly used for enriching soil, vetch is an important pollen plant for bees and other insects. It's also a food plant for quite a few butterfly and moth caterpillars, and so provides sustenance for insectivorous birds.

Vetch also offers some forage for geese, quail, and grouse. Sharp-tailed Grouse often bring their broods to take cover and feed in habitats that include American vetch.

TIGER SWALLOWTAIL

HUMMINGBIRD MOTH

USES
- Soil restoration
- Ground cover
- Prairie restoration

EXPOSURE: Sun to part shade

SOIL MOISTURE: Average

MOST USEFUL SEASON(S): Spring to fall

COLOR(S): Flowers white, pink, purple, blue

MAXIMUM HEIGHT: 3 feet (1 m)

NATIVE RANGE

RECOMMENDED SPECIES

American vetch (*Vicia americana*) can grow on disturbed soil to restore habitat, and it's one of the few native legumes adapted for arid terrain. Louisiana vetch (*V. ludoviciana*), Florida vetch (*V. floridana*), Carolina vetch (*V. caroliniana*), and other natives may be useful as ground cover, too.

Unfortunately, vetch species originally transplanted here from other continents can be very invasive. Cow or bird vetch (*V. cracca*) is pretty and feeds a variety of insects, but it grows over native plants, blocking their access to light, and crowds them out.

Sharp-tailed Grouse bring their young to feed and rest in areas where there is American vetch.

HERBACEOUS PLANTS
Perennials and Annuals

Backyard landscaping projects usually involve fewer species of trees and shrubs than annuals and perennials. A good variety of herbaceous plants can support many species of birds over a wide stretch of time, from early spring through late fall and even winter.

Aster
Aster, Eurybia, Symphyotrichum

Beebalm
Monarda

Black-eyed Susan
Rudbeckia

Blanketflower
Gaillardia

Blazing Star
Liatris

California Fuchsia
Epilobium

Cardinal Flower
Lobelia

Columbine
Aquilegia

Cup Plant, Compass Plant, Rosinweed
Silphium

Fireweed
Chamerion

Goldenrod
Solidago

Hyssop
Agastache

Iris
Iris

Ironweed
Vernonia

Jewelweed
Impatiens

Joe-Pye Weed
Eutrochium, formerly *Eupatorium*

Lily
Lilium

Lupine
Lupinus

Mexican Hat
Ratibida

Milkweed
Asclepias

Penstemon, Beardtongue
Penstemon

Phlox
Phlox

Purple Coneflower
Echinacea

Rocky Mountain Bee Plant
Cleome

Salvia
Salvia

Strawberry
Fragaria

Sunflower
Helianthus

Thistle
Cirsium

Violet
Viola

Wild Geranium
Geranium

ALPINE ASTER

ROUGHLEAF ASTER

37 Aster

Aster, Eurybia, Symphyotrichum

Most native North American asters, now classified in the *Eurybia* and *Symphyotrichum* genera, are extremely valuable for birds, providing large, nutritious seeds and hosting a great many caterpillars. Some asters are threatened or endangered.

Alpine aster is our only native member of the genus *Aster*. It's very important for insect pollinators and provides food for both insectivorous and seed-eating birds. It is considered critically imperiled in Colorado and Wyoming.

RECOMMENDED SPECIES

Alpine aster (*Aster alpinus*) is a truly alpine species, needing a cool climate. Any locally native *Eurybia* asters are excellent choices for a bird garden.

continued on next page **119**

NATIVE RANGE

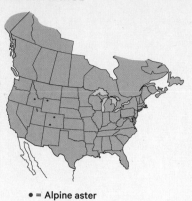

• = Alpine aster

USES

- Hedgerow
- Wildflower meadow/prairie restoration
- Ornamental
- Ground cover

EXPOSURE: Sun, part shade, shade

SOIL MOISTURE: Dry to moist, well drained

MOST USEFUL SEASON(S): Late spring to late fall depending on species

COLOR(S): Lavender or lavender-pink with yellow center, white, blue, purple, pink

MAXIMUM HEIGHT: 1 to 4 feet (0.3 to 1.2 m) depending on genus

NORTHERN CARDINAL

Heartleaf aster (*Symphyotrichum cordifolium*) can be found on open wooded slopes, along the banks of streams, on moist ledges, in swampy woods, and along the borders of beech-maple and oak-hickory forests, as well as in clearings, in thickets, and along roadsides and ditches. It can also show up in urban areas where people who don't know better call it a weed.

Silky aster or western silver aster (*S. sericeum*), native to the central plains, has the largest flowers for its size; it's listed as Rare in Indiana and Threatened in Michigan. Barrens silky aster (*S. pratense*), of the Southeast, is listed as Threatened in Arkansas and Tennessee and of Special Concern in Kentucky. Despite its name, New England aster (*S. novae-angliae*) has a fairly wide range. New York aster (*S. novi-belgii*) is much more limited to the eastern provinces and states.

38

Beebalm

Monarda

Several species of beebalm and wild bergamot, all native to North America, provide superb nectar for hummingbirds as well as for bees, butterflies, and moths. They also are primary food plants for some caterpillars, providing additional food for insectivores. They establish quickly.

RECOMMENDED SPECIES

Most beebalm and bergamot species are found in the East, such as scarlet beebalm (*Monarda didyma*) and spotted beebalm (*M. punctata*). Wild bergamot (*M. fistulosa*) ranges more widely. Lemon beebalm (*M. citriodora*), found in the South and Southwest, tolerates dry and sandy soils. Different species vary in moisture needs, so make sure to find locally native species.

RUBY-THROATED HUMMINGBIRD

USES
- Hummingbird garden
- Prairie restoration/wildflower meadow
- Ornamental

EXPOSURE: Sun to part shade

SOIL MOISTURE: Average to dry

MOST USEFUL SEASON(S): Summer

COLOR(S): Lavender, red, purple, white, pink

MAXIMUM HEIGHT: 4 feet (1.2 m)

NATIVE

39 Black-eyed Susan

Rudbeckia

Along with other coneflowers belonging to *Rudbeckia,* black-eyed Susans support caterpillars and the birds that eat them, and they produce seeds relished by cardinals, titmice and chickadees, goldfinches, towhees, sparrows, and more. Most *Rudbeckia* species grow easily from seeds.

The black-eyed Susan, the state flower of Maryland, blooms in late summer and early autumn. The winning horse in the Preakness Stakes, run in Baltimore, traditionally wears a blanket of Viking poms (a chrysanthemum) because real black-eyed Susans aren't in bloom when the race is run in May.

USES
- Prairie restoration/wildflower meadow
- Wetland restoration
- Reclaimed industrial land
- Pasture/rangeland
- Ornamental

EXPOSURE: Sun

SOIL MOISTURE: Dry to wet, depending on species

MOST USEFUL SEASON(S): Summer

COLOR(S): Yellow

MAXIMUM HEIGHT: 6+ feet (1.8+ m)

NATIVE RANGE

RECOMMENDED SPECIES
The black-eyed Susan (*Rudbeckia hirta*) ranges widely, especially in the eastern and prairie states and provinces. Orange coneflower (*R. fulgida*) is a bit more restricted to the East. Most black-eyed Susans are native in the East or prairie states, but western coneflower (*R. occidentalis*) and California coneflower (*R. californica*) are among the choices in the West.

BALTIMORE ORIOLE

40 Blanketflower

Gaillardia

Drought-tolerant, colorful, and long-blooming, blanketflowers attract insectivores to consume both the caterpillars and the flying insects these plants host. Their seeds provide food for many birds, too, such as titmice and chickadees, House Finches, and goldfinches.

RECOMMENDED SPECIES

Of the dozen or so *Gaillardia* species native to North America, the two that are easiest to find in garden stores are blanketflower (*G. aristata*), a perennial, and Indian blanket or firewheel (*G. pulchella*), an annual that easily self-seeds. Indian blanket is the state flower of Oklahoma.

Some blanketflowers are important local native plants, such as lanceleaf blanketflower (*G. aestivalis*), native to the south-central and southern United States. A rare variety, white fireweed (*G. aestivalis* var. *winkleri*), is endemic to the Pineywoods of Texas. The Arizona blanketflower (*G. arizonica*) is found in Arizona, southwestern Utah, and southern Nevada into the Sonora Desert in northwestern Mexico.

HOUSE FINCH

AMERICAN LADY BUTTERFLY

NATIVE RANGE

USES
- Prairie restoration/ wildflower meadow
- Pasture/rangeland
- Ornamental

EXPOSURE: Sun

SOIL MOISTURE: Average to dry

MOST USEFUL SEASON(S): Summer, early fall

COLOR(S): Orange, red, yellow

MAXIMUM HEIGHT: 2+ feet (0.6+ m)

41 Blazing Star

Liatris

The many species of blazing star, all native to North America, are important food sources for several caterpillars that, in turn, feed many insectivorous birds. The nectar-rich flowers attract butterflies, and they hold a special attraction for feeding monarchs.

Hummingbirds occasionally visit, too. Goldfinches and chickadees are among the small birds that feed on the seeds, and bluebirds are attracted to the plants for insects. Plants belonging to *Liatris* are also called "gayfeathers" for the feathery appearance of their blossoms.

MONARCH BUTTERFLY

USES

- Hummingbird garden
- Prairie restoration/wildflower meadow
- Ornamental

EXPOSURE: Sun

SOIL MOISTURE: Dry to moist

MOST USEFUL SEASON(S): Summer

COLOR(S): Lavender

MAXIMUM HEIGHT: 6 feet (1.8 m)

NATIVE RANGE

RECOMMENDED SPECIES

Meadow blazing star (*Liatris ligulistylis*) is widespread in the central provinces and central states. Rough or tall blazing star (*L. aspera*) is found in the East. Cattail gayfeather (*L. pycnostachya*) is listed as Threatened in Indiana. That species and marsh or dense blazing star (*L. spicata*) both do well in wet areas.

Blazing stars are closely related to *Garberia*, a genus with just one species (*G. heterophylla*), a shrub endemic to northern and central Florida.

EASTERN BLUEBIRD

AMERICAN GOLDFINCH

CALIFORNIA FUCHSIA

FUCHSIA-FLOWERED GOOSEBERRY

California Fuchsia

Epilobium

True fuchsias, belonging to the genus *Fuchsia*, are native to South and Central America as far north as Mexico. Two unrelated native North American species, both found mainly or entirely in California, are also called fuchsias.

The beautiful California fuchsia, nicknamed the hummingbird trumpet, is actually a member of the evening primrose family along with willowherbs. Blossoming in July and August, it provides a primary source of nectar for hummingbirds in the summer months.

The unrelated fuchsia-flowered gooseberry, sometimes confusingly also called the California fuchsia, is native to central and southern California. Some ornithologists believe that winter breeding in

ANNA'S HUMMINGBIRD

CALIFORNIA FUCHSIA

USES
- Ornamental

EXPOSURE: Full sun or light shade

SOIL MOISTURE: Well drained

MOST USEFUL SEASON(S): Summer

COLOR(S): Orange, red

MAXIMUM HEIGHT: 3 feet (1 m)

NATIVE RANGE

Anna's Hummingbird and this plant evolved together. The fruits and seeds are important for a great many other birds as well.

RECOMMENDED SPECIES

California fuchsia (*Epilobium canum*) is ideal for gardeners who want blossoms in summer. It's native in foothills and coastal areas, and it depends on hummingbirds for pollination.

Other plants belonging to the genus *Epilobium*, some called willowherbs, do host native insects but aren't as attractive to birds.

Fuchsia-flowered gooseberry (*Ribes speciosum*), entirely unrelated despite having somewhat similar flowers and needing hummingbirds for pollination, loses its leaves in summer during droughts and should be planted in part shade. This thorny shrub, which can reach 12 feet (3.6 m), blooms from January into May.

Allen's Hummingbird is one of many species attracted to the red flowers of California fuchsia.

43 | Cardinal Flower

Lobelia

Although *Lobelia* includes a great many native flowering plants, just one, the cardinal flower, has specific value for birds. Found naturally in wet places such as streambanks and swamps, cardinal flowers fuel Ruby-throated Hummingbird migration, the flowers' bright red color attracting the attention of hummers passing through.

Adult male Ruby-throated Hummingbirds begin their migration south in July as cardinal flowers begin to bloom. The blossoms continue as adult females and then the young of the year migrate, providing nectar and insects to nourish hummingbirds into September.

RUBY-THROATED
HUMMINGBIRD

RECOMMENDED SPECIES

Cardinal flower (*Lobelia cardinalis*) is found throughout eastern North America, and in the West south of Nebraska and Colorado to California.

NATIVE RANGE

USES
- Prairie restoration/wildflower meadow
- Wetland restoration
- Ornamental

EXPOSURE: Sun to part shade

SOIL MOISTURE: Average to wet

MOST USEFUL SEASON(S): Mid- to late summer

COLOR(S): Red

MAXIMUM HEIGHT: 28 inches (71 cm)

44 Columbine

Aquilegia

Very important for caterpillars and the birds that feed on them, columbines take both their common and scientific names from birds. The word *columbine* is derived from Latin for "dove" (the dove family is *Columbidae*) due to the resemblance of the inverted flower to five doves in a cluster; the genus name *Aquilegia* is from the Latin word for "eagle" (*aquila*) because the flower petals somewhat resemble an eagle's talons.

Both yellow and blue columbines—such as the Colorado blue columbine (*A. caerulea*, the state flower of Colorado)—are specially adapted to be pollinated by hawk moths; their nectar isn't easily available for hummingbirds. But the red columbines are

RUBY-THROATED HUMMINGBIRD

USES
- Ornamental
- Wildflower garden

EXPOSURE: Shade and part shade

SOIL MOISTURE: Dry to moist but well drained

MOST USEFUL SEASON(S): Spring through fall; year-round where temperatures are mild

COLOR(S): Red, pink, blue, yellow

MAXIMUM HEIGHT: 20 inches (51 cm)

NATIVE RANGE

adapted for hummingbird pollination: The nectar has a higher sugar content and the flower's shape makes it easily accessible.

RECOMMENDED SPECIES

Eastern red columbine (*Aquilegia canadensis*), the only columbine east of the 100th meridian, is found throughout the entire breeding range of the Ruby-throated Hummingbird. The insects on wild columbine of all species attract many small insectivorous birds, and the seeds attract goldfinches, Indigo Buntings, and Purple Finches, among others. Crimson columbine (*A. formosa*) is primarily pollinated by sphinx moths, but hummingbirds are attracted to it as well.

INDIGO BUNTING

45 Cup Plant, Compass Plant, Rosinweed

Silphium

Seed-eating birds swarm to cup plants, which produce fairly large seeds relished by a wide range of species. *Silphium* also attracts pollinators, including large, stunning butterflies; their caterpillars provide yet another food source for birds.

The leaves of cup plant form a cup that fills with water after a rain, attracting a great many small birds to drink. Compass plant and the rosinweeds produce sap thick enough that, when hardened, can be chewed like gum. These plants are typically pollinated by bees and butterflies, but hummingbirds occasionally join in—especially at cup plants—attracted to tiny insects and water as well as to the nectar.

The sturdy leaves and deep taproot of cup plants make them tough and long lived, but also difficult to transplant. They grow best from seeds or shoots off the parent plant.

RECOMMENDED SPECIES

Silphium species have declined with the loss of native prairie, but cup plant (*S. perfoliatum*) can grow densely enough in fertile, moist soils that it's considered potentially invasive in Connecticut even as it's listed as Threatened in Michigan. Compass plant (*S. laciniatum*) takes its name from the way its huge leaves orient to face north or south, avoiding the midday sun. Starry rosinweed (*S. asteriscus*) is native in the Deep South. Flower stalks of prairie dock (*S. terebinthinaceum*) can reach 10 feet (3 m).

Birds often drink rainwater from the leaf cups.

CUP PLANT, COMPASS PLANT, ROSINWEED

USES
- Prairie restoration/wildflower meadow
- Pasture/rangeland
- Ornamental

EXPOSURE: Sun

SOIL MOISTURE: Moist to dry; drought tolerant

MOST USEFUL SEASON(S): Summer and fall

COLOR(S): Yellow

MAXIMUM HEIGHT: 10 feet (3 m)

NATIVE RANGE

46 Fireweed

Chamerion

A pioneer species of the northern and mountain states through Canada, fireweed often pops up naturally following fires and clear-cuts and is the official floral emblem of the Yukon Territory. It's an important hummingbird flower, and it hosts caterpillars, thus providing food for insectivores.

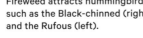

Fireweed attracts hummingbirds, such as the Black-chinned (right) and the Rufous (left).

USES
- Hummingbird garden
- Prairie restoration/wildflower meadow
- Hedgerow
- Ornamental

EXPOSURE: Sun to part shade

SOIL MOISTURE: Average

MOST USEFUL SEASON(S): Summer into fall

COLOR(S): Pink

MAXIMUM HEIGHT: 6 feet (1.8 m)

NATIVE RANGE

Living up to its name, fireweed was one of the first plants to appear after the eruption of Mount Saint Helens in 1980. It's native throughout the temperate Northern Hemisphere; in Britain and Ireland it's called rosebay willowherb or Saint Anthony's laurel. During World War II, this plant grew so quickly in bomb craters that it was nicknamed bombweed. J. R. R. Tolkien mentioned it growing where a bonfire had burned the Old Forest in *The Fellowship of the Ring*.

RECOMMENDED SPECIES

Originally placed in the genus *Epilobium* with fuchsias, fireweed (*Chamerion angustifolium*) is widespread, reaching its optimal height in the Pacific Northwest. The seeds of fireweed and related plants are too tiny to work with easily, so the plants are usually available as root or rhizome cuttings.

SAVANNAH SPARROW

MONARCH BUTTERFLY

47 Goldenrod

Solidago

Many of us think of goldenrod as a weed, and hay fever sufferers often confuse it with ragweed. Ragweed pollen is indeed a common allergen, and ragweed blooms at the same time, but goldenrod is completely benign. It provides a rich supply of caterpillars for birds, and many species such as Swamp Sparrows and Pine Siskins feed on the seeds.

RECOMMENDED SPECIES

All goldenrods offer a wealth of insects and seeds for birds. Generic goldenrod is the state flower of Kentucky and Nebraska and once was the state flower of Alabama. Tall goldenrod (*Solidago gigantea*) is the state flower of South Carolina and sweet goldenrod (*S. odora*) the state flower of Delaware. Sweet

SWAMP SPARROW

WHITE-CROWNED SPARROW

HOODED OWLET CATERPILLAR

goldenrod is listed as Threatened in New Hampshire, Vermont, and Ohio. Zigzag goldenrod (*S. flexicaulis*) is listed as Threatened in Rhode Island, and showy goldenrod (*S. speciosa*) is Threatened in Maryland.

Canada goldenrod (*S. altissima*) is very widespread in North America and has become naturalized in other parts of the world. Baby or dwarf goldenrod (*S. nana*) is native to deserts and mountainsides in the western United States.

GOLDENROD

USES
- Prairie restoration/ wildflower meadow
- Land reclamation
- Pasture/rangeland
- Ornamental

EXPOSURE: Sun to part shade

SOIL MOISTURE: Average

MOST USEFUL SEASON(S): Late summer, fall

COLOR(S): Yellow

MAXIMUM HEIGHT: 6+ feet (1.8+ m)

NATIVE RANGE

48 Hyssop

Agastache

True hyssops, belonging to the genus *Hyssopus*, are not native to North America. The native species that are called hyssops on this continent belong to the genus *Agastache*. They're extremely attractive to butterflies and bees, and also to hummingbirds, especially in the Southwest.

RECOMMENDED SPECIES

When gardening for birds, focus on native plants. Purple giant hyssop (*Agastache rugosa*) is often sold but is not native to North America. Anise or giant hyssop (*A. foeniculum*) is perhaps the showiest of our native mints, found throughout much of Canada and the northern half of the United States.

Western giant hyssop (*A. occidentalis*) is native in Oregon and Washington; Texas hummingbird mint (*A. cana*) in Texas; threadleaf giant hyssop (*A. rupestris*) in Arizona and New Mexico; and nettleleaf giant hyssop (*A. urticifolia*) from British Columbia south to California and east to Montana, Wyoming, and Colorado.

RUBY-THROATED HUMMINGBIRD

NATIVE RANGE

USES
- Prairie restoration/ wildflower meadow
- Farm edges
- Ornamental
- Edible/herbal

EXPOSURE: Sun, part shade, shade

SOIL MOISTURE: Average

MOST USEFUL SEASON(S): Summer

COLOR(S): Purple, white, gold, yellow, red, pink

MAXIMUM HEIGHT: 6+ feet (1.8+ m)

TEXAS HUMMINGBIRD MINT

ANISE HYSSOP

NETTLELEAF GIANT HYSSOP

49

Iris

Iris

   ⚠ **NONNATIVES AGGRESSIVE**

The Greek word for rainbow and the Greek goddess of the rainbow give the iris its name. Many insects feed on iris, including many larvae, so the plant is a good food source for insectivores. Hummingbirds visit for nectar as well as insects.

Yellow iris (*Iris pseudacorus*), an invasive exotic species from Europe, western Asia, and northwest Africa, has been cultivated in North America, especially for water purification in wet areas where agricultural runoff is a problem; yellow iris consumes nutrient pollutants. As with so many other invasive exotics, though, yellow iris is highly aggressive, clogging natural waterways and outcompeting native plants. It's now banned in some states and should never be part of a North American bird-scaping plan.

RUBY-THROATED HUMMINGBIRD ON BLUE FLAG

RECOMMENDED SPECIES

Blue flag (*Iris versicolor*), the provincial flower of Quebec, is a showy native plant of northeastern wetlands. Southern blue flag or Virginia iris (*I. virginica*) occurs from Virginia to Florida and Texas. Slender blue flag (*I. prismatica*), which is found mostly in coastal, brackish water from Maine to Georgia, has extremely narrow, grasslike leaves. Western blue flag (*I. missouriensis*) and tough-leaf iris (*I. tenax*) are two of the irises native in the western part of the continent.

Irises are highly toxic—grazing on them can kill calves—so should never be planted near livestock pastures.

Many insectivorous birds, such as Common Yellowthroats, feed on the insects hosted by irises.

IRIS

USES
- Ornamental
- Rain garden
- Prairie restoration

EXPOSURE: Sun to part shade

SOIL MOISTURE: Dry to moist, depending on species

MOST USEFUL SEASON(S): Spring to midsummer

COLOR(S): Blue, purple, pink

MAXIMUM HEIGHT: 3 feet (1 m)

NATIVE RANGE

50

Ironweed

Vernonia

Although its direct value to birds is somewhat limited, ironweed hosts several species of insect larvae and attracts butterflies and other flying insects that birds then feed on. Its nectar sometimes draws hummingbirds, and its seeds bring a wide variety of birds such as American Goldfinches, House Finches, and Song Sparrows. It's an aggressive grower so can take over small gardens quickly.

RECOMMENDED SPECIES

Some good choices include prairie ironweed (*Vernonia fasciculata*), New York ironweed (*V. noveboracensis*), and Missouri ironweed (*V. missurica*). Tall or giant ironweed (*V. gigantea*) is listed as Endangered in New York.

HOUSE FINCH

NATIVE RANGE

USES
- Wildflower meadow
- Wetland restoration
- Ornamental

EXPOSURE: Sun

SOIL MOISTURE: Average to wet

MOST USEFUL SEASON(S): Summer

COLOR(S): Purple

MAXIMUM HEIGHT: 7 feet (2 m)

51 Jewelweed
Impatiens

The nectar-rich flowers of orange jewelweed are especially attractive to hummingbirds, its primary pollinators. It also hosts caterpillars that support insectivores.

The seed pods open at the slightest touch. People who grew up with jewelweed, however, often describe how as children they learned to remove the seed pods carefully, place them in their mouths, then wait for the "pop!" and the English walnut taste.

Birds such as Ruffed Grouse and Northern Bobwhites also feed on the seeds, though we haven't discovered whether their young also make a game of it.

Jewelweed is one of the few native plants that successfully competes with invasive garlic mustard.

NORTHERN BOBWHITE

continued on next page

Ruffed Grouse are among the birds that feed on jewelweed seeds. Humans use the juice of jewelweed to soothe nettle stings and poison ivy or poison oak itch.

RECOMMENDED SPECIES

Of North America's five native species of *Impatiens*, orange jewelweed (*I. capensis*) is the one with an important place in a bird garden, because of its value for hummingbirds. Although it's an annual, it self-seeds, and in a shady, wet spot it may spread aggressively.

The other native *Impatiens* species are pollinated by insects.

JEWELWEED

NATIVE RANGE

USES
- Ornamental
- Ground cover

EXPOSURE: Shade to part shade

SOIL MOISTURE: Moist, wet

MOST USEFUL SEASON(S): Late summer, early fall

COLOR(S): Orange, yellow

MAXIMUM HEIGHT: 5 feet (1.5 m)

52 Joe-Pye Weed

Eutrochium, formerly *Eupatorium*

Even though the word *weed* is baked into Joe-Pye weed's very name, it's a native plant with a great many benefits to birds. It hosts a wonderful diversity of both larval and adult insects—essential food for insectivorous birds—and also provides seeds for many small birds such as titmice, goldfinches, and juncos.

The plant takes its name from folklore. A Colonial-era healer named Joe Pye is said to have used the coastal-plain plant to cure fevers, and early colonists used it to treat an outbreak of typhus.

MONARCH BUTTERFLY

TUFTED TITMOUSE

147

RECOMMENDED SPECIES

Several species native to the eastern two-thirds of the continent are called Joe-Pye weeds, and all host an abundance of insects. Spotted Joe-Pye weed (*Eutrochium maculatum*), also called spotted trumpet-weed, is widespread. The foliage of sweet Joe-Pye weed (*E. purpureum*) smells like vanilla when crushed. Hollow Joe-Pye weed (*E. fistulosum*) has a hollow stem. The plant first named "Joe-Pye weed" is the coastal plain Joe-Pye weed (*E. dubium*), also called eastern Joe-Pye weed, which is listed as Threatened in Maine.

Taxonomic fluctuations can make choosing Joe-Pye weeds confusing, because some botanists place some of the plants in different genera such as *Eupatorium* and *Eupatoriadelphus*. "Boneset" plants (so named because the stem appears to be growing through the leaf, which indicated to some early doctors that the plant would be useful in setting bones) also belong to *Eupatorium*. Like the other Joe-Pye weeds, these are native and host a wide variety of seed- and insect-eating birds.

A goldfinch feasts on Joe-Pye weed seeds.

JOE-PYE WEED

NATIVE RANGE

USES
- Prairie restoration/wildflower meadow
- Wetland restoration
- Ornamental
- Rain garden

EXPOSURE: Sun to part shade

SOIL MOISTURE: Average to wet

MOST USEFUL SEASON(S): Summer

COLOR(S): Pink, purple

MAXIMUM HEIGHT: 7 feet (2.1 m)

53

Lily

Lilium

  ⚠ ATTRACT DEER;
DAYLILIES INVASIVE

The many insects that lilies attract bring warblers, waxwings, and other insectivores. Hummingbirds visit these flowers for nectar as well as for tiny insects. The western lily produces more nectar than any other native lily, specifically to attract hummingbirds, its primary pollinators.

Over much of their range in North America, lilies are declining. One major reason is the large increase in white-tailed deer, which consume lilies in preference to other foods.

Daylilies, which are neither native nor true lilies (they belong to the genus *Hemerocallis*), were introduced from Asia as ornamentals. They can be invasive both in the wild and in a backyard garden. Except for the North American lily of the valley (*Convallaria*), endemic in the lower Appalachians and listed as Endangered in Kentucky, other plants belonging to *Convallaria* hail from Asia and Europe and don't really belong in a bird garden.

continued on next page

WOOD LILY

TROUT LILY

NATIVE RANGE

USES
- Ornamental

EXPOSURE: Sun to shade

SOIL MOISTURE: Moist

MOST USEFUL SEASON(S): Mid- to late summer

COLOR(S): Orange, yellow

MAXIMUM HEIGHT: 6 feet (1.8 m)

Most birds that benefit from lilies, like this Cedar Waxwing, don't feed on the plants directly, but instead snap up insects attracted to the plants.

RECOMMENDED SPECIES

Any locally native lily is an excellent choice. Unfortunately, deer will almost certainly be attracted and will also feed on other nearby plants. If you grow lilies where deer are a problem, fences as high as 8 feet (2.4 m) may be necessary.

Western lily (*Lilium occidentale*) is listed as Endangered in California and Oregon; Michigan lily (*L. michiganense*) as Endangered in New York and Threatened in Tennessee; and Turk's-cap lily (*L. superbum*) as Endangered in Florida and New Hampshire, Threatened in Kentucky, and Exploitably Vulnerable in New York. A wide assortment of hummingbirds are attracted to locally native southwestern lilies. These include the very rare lemon lily (*L. parryi*), native to southern California and Arizona, where it's listed as Salvage Restricted.

54

Lupine

Lupinus

⚠ BIGLEAF LUPINE
INVASIVE IN EAST

Hummingbirds are sometimes attracted to lupines, but the plant's role as host for many butterfly caterpillars, most notably for various endemic blue butterflies, means it also offers an abundance of native insects for insectivores. A variety of other birds eat lupine seeds, and the plant provides cover and nest sites as well.

Unfortunately, the beautiful bigleaf lupine, native to the American West, has become an invasive weed in much of the East.

KARNER BLUE
BUTTERFLY

RECOMMENDED SPECIES

Perennial or sundial lupine (*Lupinus perennis*) is the most widely distributed native lupine in the East, growing best in sandy, deep soil. This is the host plant of the endangered Karner blue butterfly. Silvery lupine (*L. argenteus*) is one of the most widely distributed lupines in the desert Southwest, Rocky Mountains, and Great Basin.

Bigleaf lupine (*L. polyphyllus*) is native from Santa Cruz County, California north to British Columbia, and east in the mountains from Alberta to Colorado. Avoid planting this species anywhere in the Midwest or the East.

Top: California Quail are especially fond of lupine seeds. **Bottom:** House Finches feed on lupine seeds and sometimes nest in the plant.

LUPINE

USES

- Prairie restoration/ wildflower meadow
- Hedgerow
- Ornamental
- Rain garden

EXPOSURE: Sun to part shade

SOIL MOISTURE: Average to dry

MOST USEFUL SEASON(S): Spring to summer

COLOR(S): Blue, purple, white, yellow

MAXIMUM HEIGHT: 6 feet (1.8 m)

NATIVE RANGE

55 Mexican Hat

Ratibida

Sometimes called prairie coneflowers, Mexican hats are beautiful flowers whose nectar attracts bees and butterflies, thus benefiting insectivorous birds. A great many seed-eating birds also devour the seeds. Mexican hats repel deer but are very aggressive and may crowd out other flowers if you don't thin them regularly.

American Goldfinches are among the many birds that feed on Mexican hats.

RECOMMENDED SPECIES

Mexican hat (*Ratibida columnifera*) is the most widespread of the plants in this genus. Naked Mexican hat (*R. peduncularis*) is found in the sandy soils of the coastal plains of Texas and Louisiana. Grayhead Mexican hat or prairie coneflower (*R. pinnata*) is a taller plant, reaching 6 feet (1.8 m), and its tall stems may need support. It has been **extirpated** (removed completely) from Pennsylvania.

MEXICAN HAT

USES
- Ornamental
- Prairie restoration/wildflower meadow

EXPOSURE: Sun to part shade

SOIL MOISTURE: Dry to moist

MOST USEFUL SEASON(S): Spring through fall

COLOR(S): Flowers orange, yellow, brown

MAXIMUM HEIGHT: 3 feet (1 m)

NATIVE RANGE

VIRGINIA CTENUCHA MOTH

56 Milkweed

Asclepias

SOME INVASIVE IN OREGON AND THE GULF

Although milkweed's association with monarch butterflies is well known, its significant value for birds may be less so. American Goldfinches not only eat the seeds and feed them to their young, but they also incorporate the downy fluff of the seeds into their tightly woven nests.

Few birds eat the caterpillars hosted by milkweed because of the toxins in the plant's leaves and milky juice. But milkweed blossoms draw many flying insects that feed insectivores, including hummingbirds, which also occasionally feed on the nectar.

RUBY-THROATED HUMMINGBIRD

USES
- Prairie restoration/ wildflower meadow
- Hedgerow
- Wetland restoration
- Ornamental

EXPOSURE: Sun

SOIL MOISTURE: Wet to dry

MOST USEFUL SEASON(S): Summer, early autumn

COLOR(S): White, purple, pink, orange, green

MAXIMUM HEIGHT: 5 feet (1.5 m)

NATIVE RANGE

RECOMMENDED SPECIES

Look for locally native species. Swamp milkweed (*Asclepias incarnata*) and whorled milkweed (*A. verticillata*) are native to most of eastern North America and parts of the West. Whitestem milkweed (*A. albicans*) and antelope horns or spider milkweed (*A. asperula*) are native to the Southwest. The range of butterfly weed (*A. tuberosa*) extends from almost the entire eastern half of the continent down into the Southwest.

Common milkweed (*A. syriaca*) is a good choice where it's native in the East, but in Oregon, where it is not native, it has become naturalized and can be invasive. And tropical milkweed (*A. curassavica*), not native to the United States or Canada, has been naturalized in the Gulf where it blooms all year, encouraging monarch butterflies to breed year-round also. This not only affects the monarch's migration patterns; it also causes dramatic population surges of a dangerous monarch parasite. It's wisest to select locally native species only.

Milkweed draws more than just monarchs. Native bees, honey bees, and hummingbird moths visit, as do hummingbirds.

57 Penstemon, Beardtongue

Penstemon

Although not particularly common anywhere, *Penstemon* is the largest genus of flowering plants endemic to North America. The species native to a given area are fairly easy to grow and are especially important in dry landscapes.

Penstemons support native caterpillars that provide food for insectivores. Chickadees and titmice, nuthatches, sparrows, and cardinals feed on the seeds, and the species with red flowers are extremely attractive to hummingbirds.

NORTHERN CARDINALS

USES
- Wildflower meadow/prairie restoration
- Hedgerow
- Ornamental

EXPOSURE: Sun to part shade

SOIL MOISTURE: Average to dry

MOST USEFUL SEASON(S): Summer

COLOR(S): White, pink, purple, red

MAXIMUM HEIGHT: 4 feet (1.2 m)

NATIVE RANGE

RECOMMENDED SPECIES

In the East, smooth or foxglove beardtongue (*Penstemon digitalis*) and large-flowered penstemon (*P. grandiflorus*) are good choices. In the West, some good options are Venus penstemon (*P. venustus*), and Palmer's penstemon (*P. palmeri*).

To invite hummingbirds, the brilliant red flowers of several penstemons are especially valuable. In Texas, Louisiana, Oklahoma, and Arkansas, scarlet penstemon (*P. murrayanus*) is ideal. In the West, Eaton's penstemon (*P. eatonii*) is an excellent choice. The late-flowering golden-beard penstemon (*P. barbatus*) blooms just as Rufous Hummingbirds are migrating south.

Local native-plant nurseries and knowledgeable gardeners will have other suggestions.

A Rufous Hummingbird forages in penstemon.

58 Phlox

Phlox

Perennial and annual phlox provide a lovely ground cover while supporting caterpillars, including those of some spectacular hummingbird moths. They are found in widely diverse habitats, from alpine tundra to open woodland, from prairie to Western scrub and sagebrush, and even in southwestern deserts. Some species' flowers attract humans for their fragrance, and some attract hummingbirds for their nectar.

Each blossom produces a single seed that sparrows, juncos, and other birds may feed on. Some birds even jump the gun and eat the flower buds.

CHIPPING SPARROW

PHLOX

USES
- Ornamental
- Ground cover

EXPOSURE: Sun or part shade

SOIL MOISTURE: Moist but well drained

MOST USEFUL SEASON(S): Summer to fall

COLOR(S): Flowers blue, violet, pink, red, white

MAXIMUM HEIGHT: 3 feet (1 m)

NATIVE RANGE

RECOMMENDED SPECIES

More than 60 species of phlox are native to North America, including many endemics found naturally in rather small ranges; some of these are listed as Threatened or Endangered. A listing of locally native species of your county or state should offer at least a few phlox that would be appropriate for your yard's growing conditions.

HUMMINGBIRD MOTH

59 Purple Coneflower

Echinacea

Like the coneflowers in other genera, *Echinacea* coneflowers host a good assortment of larvae for insectivorous birds and produce seeds attractive to goldfinches and many other seed-eating species. *Echinacea* is harvested so intensively for various folk medicines that it's listed as Threatened in Tennessee and Wisconsin.

Like many other grassland birds, Eastern Meadowlarks feed on both the insects hosted and the seeds produced by purple coneflowers.

RECOMMENDED SPECIES

Purple coneflowers are found in the eastern and central states and southeastern Canada. Common purple coneflower (*Echinacea purpurea*) is the easiest to find for purchase. Other choices, where available, are narrow-leaved purple coneflower (*E. angustifolia*) and pale purple coneflower (*E. pallida*). These are slow-growing plants, but once established they are very long lived.

Indigo Buntings look for caterpillars to feed their young just as coneflowers are in bloom.

PURPLE CONEFLOWER

USES
- Prairie restoration/wildflower meadow
- Pasture/rangeland
- Ornamental

EXPOSURE: Sun

SOIL MOISTURE: Average

MOST USEFUL SEASON(S): Summer

COLOR(S): Purple

MAXIMUM HEIGHT: 4 feet (1.2 m)

NATIVE RANGE

60 Rocky Mountain Bee Plant

Cleome

As their name suggests, bee plants are important sources of nectar for bees, but butterflies (including monarchs), moths, and hummingbirds also drink from them. They grow well on disturbed soils, tolerating soil and climate conditions where few other plants grow, so are regionally very important. They offer cover for many ground-nesting and roosting birds, and their seeds provide valuable food for doves and other ground birds.

RECOMMENDED SPECIES

Bee plants are found in Western states and provinces except along the Pacific slope and in southern Arizona and New Mexico. The pink-flowered Rocky Mountain bee plant (*Cleome serrulata*) is a great choice for restoring overgrazed or otherwise disturbed rangeland where it's not too dry. The yellow bee plant (*C. lutea*) can even be grown on very dry alkaline soils.

NATIVE RANGE

USES
- Hedgerow
- Prairie restoration/ wildflower meadow
- Pasture/rangeland
- Ornamental

EXPOSURE: Sun

SOIL MOISTURE: Wet to dry

MOST USEFUL SEASON(S): Summer

COLOR(S): Purple, pink, yellow

MAXIMUM HEIGHT: 6 feet (1.8 m)

Bee plants provide nectar to hummingbirds as well as bees, and they also offer cover for many ground-nesting and roosting birds.

MOURNING DOVE

HORNED LARK

WESTERN MEADOWLARK

FRAGRANT SAGE

61

Salvia

Salvia

Belonging to the mint family and often called sages, salvias can grow as shrubs, smaller perennials, and annuals. Rosemary and sage both belong to the genus. It's far wiser to select native than nonnative species, because some tropical salvias grown in the United States may be affecting the wintering ranges of some migratory hummingbirds.

RECOMMENDED SPECIES

Native salvias attractive to hummingbirds include two California natives, the perennial hummingbird sage (*Salvia spathacea*) and the shrubbier fragrant sage (*S. clevelandii*). One southeastern Arizona and Mexico native is baby sage (*S. microphylla*). Two Texas natives that are also hummingbird magnets are the perennial autumn sage (*S. greggii*) and the shrubby royal sage (*S. regla*). A couple of salvias native to California, the Great Basin of Utah, Oregon, and

RUFOUS HUMMINGBIRD ON HUMMINGBIRD SAGE

Native salvias attractive to hummingbirds include two California natives, the perennial hummingbird sage (bottom) and the shrubbier fragrant sage (top).

USES
- Hedgerow
- Pasture/rangeland
- Ornamental

EXPOSURE: Sun

SOIL MOISTURE: Average to dry

MOST USEFUL SEASON(S): Summer

COLOR(S): Blue, purple, pink, red, white

MAXIMUM HEIGHT: 4 feet (1.2 m)

NATIVE RANGE

Nevada, *S. pachyphylla* and *S. dorrii*, can also be excellent choices.

Lanceleaf sage (*S. reflexa*) has the widest range of North American sages, extending through most of the Lower 48 states except the Southeast, New England, Washington, and Idaho.

One salvia often called hummingbird sage (*S. guaranitica*) is an exotic, native to South America.

SCARLET SAGE

White-crowned Sparrows are among the host of birds that feed on salvia seeds.

62 Strawberry

Fragaria

More than 50 bird species feed on native strawberries, including prairie chickens, turkeys, and quail; jays and crows; catbirds, thrashers, and mockingbirds; robins and other thrushes; and sparrows and towhees. But strawberry plants sustain birds in other significant ways, too: They host a huge number of caterpillars that in turn support insectivorous birds.

When you grow cultivated varieties of strawberries for your own consumption, you'll feel less guilty about caging them with bird netting if you also grow native strawberries for the birds. Remember to make bird netting taut to avoid entangling visiting birds.

USES
- Ground cover
- Ornamental
- Edible fruits

EXPOSURE: Sun, part sun, shade

SOIL MOISTURE: Dry to medium

MOST USEFUL SEASON(S): Spring, summer

COLOR(S): Flowers white; fruits red

MAXIMUM HEIGHT: 1 foot (0.3 m)

NATIVE RANGE

RECOMMENDED SPECIES

Finding a locally native strawberry for your yard shouldn't be too difficult. Two widespread species are wild strawberry (*Fragaria virginiana*) and American woodland strawberry (*F. vesca* ssp. *americana*). A good choice for California and Oregon is *F. vesca* ssp. *californica*.

GRAY CATBIRD

Many birds walk on lawns searching for wild strawberries.

BLUE JAY

BROWN THRASHER

63 Sunflower

Helianthus

Almost entirely native to North and Central America, sunflowers are best known for their seeds, which supply abundant food for a wide variety of seed-eating birds, both at feeders and on the flowers. Sunflowers also host a great many caterpillars, making them equally important for insectivores.

Gardeners often plant Jerusalem artichoke (*Helianthus tuberosus,* a sunflower species not associated in any way with Jerusalem nor related to artichokes) because it's so attractive to aphids that it draws them from other garden plants. This is good not only for the garden plants but also for tiny insectivorous birds, including hummingbirds, that feed on the aphids.

RUBY-THROATED HUMMINGBIRD

USES

- Hedgerow
- Wildflower meadow/ prairie restoration
- Reclaimed land/tough sites
- Rain garden
- Pasture/rangeland
- Ornamental

EXPOSURE: Sun to shade

SOIL MOISTURE: Average to dry

MOST USEFUL SEASON(S): Late summer to autumn

COLOR(S): Yellow, orange

MAXIMUM HEIGHT: 8 feet (2.4 m)

NATIVE RANGE

RECOMMENDED SPECIES

The common sunflower (*Helianthus annuus*), native to the entire Lower 48, is the one most often grown for its seeds. Jerusalem artichoke (*H. tuberosus*), found over most of the continent except the desert Southwest, does well in rain gardens. The whorled sunflower (*H. verticillatus*) has a small range in Alabama, Georgia, and Tennessee, where it's listed as Endangered.

AMERICAN GOLDFINCH

Saving Sunflower Seed for Winter Feeding

If you want to reserve some sunflower seeds for your feeder (rather than allowing the birds to eat them on the plant), you'll need to monitor seed formation and cover flowers while they're still in bloom, before the flower starts drying and the seeds ripen. Cheesecloth, fine pliable screen, or polyspun garden fleece will allow air and light into the sunflower heads while keeping birds and squirrels out. Cut the material into a square large enough to loosely cover the flower and the top 3 or 4 inches (8 or 10 cm) of the stalk. Secure it with a loosely tied string or twist tie.

To harvest the ripe seeds, usually 30 to 45 days after the flower opens (peek to make sure the back of the flower head has turned brown), cut the flower head 4 to 12 inches (10 to 30 cm) down the stalk, with the cover still in place. To separate the seeds from the flower, unwrap the head on a work surface large enough to collect the seeds that fall into the cover material.

AMERICAN GOLDFINCH

64

Thistle

Cirsium

 **NONNATIVES INVASIVE**

Gardeners often disparage thistles, and some states classify them as noxious weeds, not realizing that *native* thistles are not a problem, and are extremely valuable to our birds and butterflies. American Goldfinches use the downy seeds as food for themselves and their young, and as building materials for their woven nests. Indigo Buntings and other small songbirds also feed voraciously on thistle seeds.

One problem species, Canada thistle (*Cirsium arvense*), isn't from Canada at all but was transplanted here from Europe and western Asia. It's also nicknamed "field thistle," but is a different species from the native field thistle (*C. discolor*). The other exotic, called bull or common thistle (*C. vulgare*), native to Europe, western Asia, and northwestern Africa, and the national flower of Scotland, is especially invasive and very unpleasant to deal with because of its sturdy, sharp spines.

American Goldfinches use native thistles (such as field thistle, top) for food and nesting material. The much thornier invasive thistles (such as bull thistle, bottom) can draw blood, so wear eye protection and heavy gloves extending up the arms when uprooting them.

USES
- Prairie restoration/wildflower meadow
- Ornamental

EXPOSURE: Sun to part shade

SOIL MOISTURE: Average to wet

MOST USEFUL SEASON(S): Summer to fall

COLOR(S): Pink, lavender, white, red

MAXIMUM HEIGHT: 8 feet (2.4 m)

NATIVE RANGE

Native thistles are not weedy and often get supplanted by invasive thistles. Unfortunately, North American birds and butterflies are attracted to invasive thistles as well as our native ones.

RECOMMENDED SPECIES

Thistle seeds and plants can be difficult to purchase except at specialty nurseries, but local native-plant gardeners may have plants or seeds to share. In the eastern and central states and provinces, field thistle (*Cirsium discolor*) is the most common native thistle. Tall thistle (*C. altissimum*), which usually grows on the edge of woodlands, lives up to its name, reaching heights of 8 feet (2.4 m).

Wavyleaf thistle (*C. undulatum*) is widespread in the western and central states and provinces. Cobweb thistle (*C. occidentale*), limited to Oregon, California, and Nevada, has brilliant red flowers.

COBWEB THISTLE

INDIGO BUNTING

PINE SISKIN

COMMON BLUE VIOLET

DOWNY YELLOW VIOLET

65 Violet
Viola

Like most native plants, violets support lots of caterpillars—they're primary hosts for beautiful fritillary butterflies—and the many native insects attracted to violets benefit insectivorous birds. Doves, quail, and grouse eat the seeds, and Wild Turkeys eat the seeds, foliage, and roots.

RECOMMENDED SPECIES

Dozens of violets are native to North America; any that are locally native are great choices for a bird garden. Local native plant experts will have good suggestions for the best species to plant for your growing conditions.

The common blue violet (*Viola sororia*) of the eastern two-thirds of the continent self-seeds freely on lawns and is considered by some to be a weed, though it's a true native and hosts native insects. The

USES

- Ornamental
- Hedgerow
- Ground cover
- Erosion control

EXPOSURE: Part shade, shade

SOIL MOISTURE: Dry, medium, or moist depending on species

MOST USEFUL SEASON(S): Spring and summer

COLOR(S): Blue, purple, yellow, white

MAXIMUM HEIGHT: 1 foot (0.3 m)

NATIVE RANGE

hooked-spur violet (*V. adunca*) is native to much of Canada and the western and northern states.

The prairie violet (*V. pedatifida*) is found in the central two-thirds of the United States and Canada; it's listed as Endangered in Ohio and Pennsylvania, and Threatened in Indiana and Michigan. Bird's-foot violet (*V. pedata*), found in the eastern half of the continent, requires sandy soil and may die if the soil stays too wet.

Left: Foraging Wild Turkeys are especially fond of native violets.

Bottom: The fritillary butterflies, such as this great spangled fritillary, depend on native violets during their larval stage. As adults, they drink nectar from a great many native plants.

66 Wild Geranium

Geranium

Usually grown for its beauty, wild geranium, or cranesbill, offers a bonus for bird lovers: It supports plenty of caterpillars. Many birds, including quail, doves, and sparrows, feed on the seeds. Wild geraniums are also visited by an assortment of bees for nectar, pollen, and nesting materials.

RECOMMENDED SPECIES

Native wild geraniums are found over the entire continent, but many nonnative imports are also sold in garden stores, so pay attention and purchase only locally native species. In the West, sticky purple geranium (*Geranium viscosissimum*) is a good choice. In the East, Bicknell's cranesbill (*G. bicknellii*) and spotted geranium or cranesbill (*G. maculatum*) are sound options.

MOURNING DOVE

GOLDEN-CROWNED SPARROW

NATIVE RANGE

USES
- Hedgerow
- Ornamental
- Reforestation
- Shade garden

EXPOSURE: Shade to part shade

SOIL MOISTURE: Average

MOST USEFUL SEASON(S): Spring

COLOR(S): White, yellow, pink, blue

MAXIMUM HEIGHT: 2 feet (0.6 m)

BICKNELL'S CRANESBILL

SPOTTED CRANESBILL

PLANTS THAT GROW ON TREES

Three plants unrelated to one another (a lichen, a sandalwood, and a bromeliad that resembles a lichen) all grow on trees, popping up as if by magic. They're seldom sold in garden stores, and few gardeners actively cultivate them—indeed, one is parasitic and ultimately kills many trees—yet all are incredibly important for birds.

Lichen
Usnea spp. and many more

Mistletoe
Phoradendron

Spanish Moss
Tillandsia

RUBY-THROATED
HUMMINGBIRDS

67 Lichen

Usnea spp. and many more

 These intriguing "composite plants," which arise from algae living within filaments of fungi, are some of the world's oldest organisms. Lichens can grow on almost any surface, including rocks, roofs, soil, and bones, and survive at all elevations from the equator to polar regions.

Although they often cover the bark, branches, and leaves of sick and dying trees, lichens are not parasitic, nor do they harm the plants they use as their substrate. People often think *Usnea* is killing their balsams and other short-lived trees, but it's

Golden-crowned Kinglets are among the small birds that incorporate lichens into their nests.

continued on next page

NATIVE RANGE

USES
- Ornamental

EXPOSURE: Sun, part shade, shade

SOIL MOISTURE: Any

MOST USEFUL SEASON(S): Spring and summer

COLOR(S): Green, yellow, red

MAXIMUM HEIGHT: Most about 1 inch (2.5 cm); clumps of *Usnea* may reach 2 feet (0.6 m) or more

Eastern Screech-Owls and other cavity nesters can often be found in older trees covered with lichens. That's because both lichens and cavities are increasingly abundant as a tree ages.

just that the lichens grow faster when they get more light through the thinning foliage of trees that were already dead or dying.

Lichens of all sorts are important for birds—not directly, by providing food, but indirectly. They indicate a clean atmosphere and offer critical nesting material for tiny birds such as hummingbirds, gnatcatchers, and kinglets. These birds construct their stretchable nests from woven spider silk, adorning them with lichens to provide structural strength and camouflage.

RECOMMENDED SPECIES

Lichens grow naturally on many substrates in backyards and gardens—unless we're too meticulous about trimming old branches. "Old man's beard" lichens (*Usnea* spp.) require clean, humid air, growing most easily within and on the edges of woods where balsams grow.

68 Mistletoe

Phoradendron

PARASITIC, MAY DAMAGE TREES

PHAINOPEPLA

A native parasitic plant belonging to the genus *Phoradendron*, mistletoe grows on the branches of a wide variety of plants, usually deciduous trees and western shrubs. It obtains water and nutrients from the host plant but is called hemiparasitic because it is photosynthetic, producing at least some of its own nutrients.

The berries on mistletoe are toxic to humans but very important for birds such as grouse, doves, waxwings, phainopeplas, robins, and blue-birds. The plant attracts many insects that birds such as House Wrens eat.

Mistletoe is one of many catalysts that cause trees to form abnormal growths of dense branches, called "witches' broom." Witches' broom is a preferred nesting site for flying squirrels and can also provide excellent nesting opportunities for hawks, owls, and a variety of songbirds.

continued on next page

A Bohemian Waxwing forages among mistletoe berries.

RECOMMENDED SPECIES

It can be tricky to buy a harmless native mistletoe. The mistletoe many people associate with Christmas kissing is a European species (*Viscum album*) not closely related to native mistletoe. Dwarf mistletoe, belonging to *Arceuthobium,* a different genus than American and oak mistletoe, is native but parasitizes mostly conifers rather than deciduous trees. It does not provide much value for wildlife relative to the serious problems it causes infected trees.

Stick to *Phoradendron*. There are several species to choose from, especially in the West. Your choice will primarily depend on what kinds of trees you want as hosts.

American mistletoe (*P. leucarpum*), the species that ranges most widely in the East, is the state floral emblem for Oklahoma. (The Oklahoma rose was named the state flower in 2004.) Christmas mistletoe (*P. tomentosum*) is the native plant that most closely resembles traditional European mistletoe, and small clumps are often used as Christmas decorations.

Big-leaf mistletoe (*P. macrophyllum*) grows in hardwood forests and woodlands in Texas, New Mexico, Arizona, and California. Mesquite mistletoe (*P. californicum*) grows in mesquite and acacia in New Mexico, Arizona, California, Nevada, and Utah. Oak mistletoe (*P. villosum*) is an important food source for birds in California and Oregon.

MISTLETOE

NATIVE RANGE

USES
• Ornamental

EXPOSURE: Sun (in trees)

SOIL MOISTURE: Not applicable

MOST USEFUL SEASON(S): Year-round

COLOR(S): Stems green, grayish green, reddish green, yellowish green; berries white

MAXIMUM HEIGHT: 5 feet (1.5 m)

69

Spanish Moss
Tillandsia

A contradiction in terms, Spanish moss is native to North America, not Spain, and not related to mosses at all. This **epiphyte** (a plant that grows upon trees without hurting them) belongs to the bromeliad family, making it a true flowering plant, although its green, brown, yellow, or gray flowers are tiny and inconspicuous.

Spanish moss produces its own nutrients and takes its water from rain and moist air, requiring the warmth and high humidity characteristic of tropical and subtropical climates. It's not parasitic, but when it grows very thickly it may cut off enough light from a supporting tree to slow its growth.

YELLOW-THROATED WARBLER

continued on next page

NATIVE RANGE

USES
- Ornamental

EXPOSURE: Shade

SOIL MOISTURE: Not applicable

MOST USEFUL SEASON(S): Year-round

COLOR(S): Gray, green; flowers green, brown, yellow, gray

MAXIMUM HEIGHT: 20 feet (6 m)

A great many birds feed on the insects associated with Spanish moss. Many use strands as nesting material, essentially propagating the Spanish moss in new trees.

Although thousands of arthropods have been identified in Spanish moss, chiggers are not associated with it.

RECOMMENDED SPECIES

Several *Tillandsia* airplants grow in the Southeast from the Carolinas through Texas, especially in Florida. Small ball moss (*T. recurvata*) is native from Louisiana to Arizona.

Spanish moss (*T. usneoides*), the most important of its genus for birds, can grow on many tree species but seems to prefer bald cypress and, especially, live oak.

Close Connection

In the hot, humid Southeast, the Northern Parula nests almost exclusively within large clumps of Spanish moss. Intriguingly, in parts of its range where Spanish moss isn't available, this tiny bird nests in "old man's beard," lichens belonging to the genus *Usnea*, which superficially resemble Spanish moss. Spanish moss's scientific name, *usneoides*, means "like usnea."

SHRUBS

Woody deciduous shrubs are among the most important plants for birds, offering an abundance of fruits, seeds, and insect food as well as excellent nesting and roosting cover. A good selection can meet other landscaping needs as well, forming privacy hedges and borders.

Beautyberry
Callicarpa

Blackberry, Raspberry
Rubus

Blueberry
Vaccinium

Buttonbush
Cephalanthus

Coralberry, Snowberry
Symphoricarpos

Crowberry
Empetrum

Desert-thorn, Wolfberry
Lycium

Dogwood
Cornus

Elderberry
Sambucus

Hawthorn
Crataegus

Hazelnut
Corylus

Holly
Ilex

Honeysuckle
Lonicera

Leadplant
Amorpha

Manzanita, Bearberry
Arctostaphylos

Rhododendron, Azalea
Rhododendron

Rose
Rosa

Sagebrush
Artemisia

Saw Palmetto
Serenoa

Serviceberry, Juneberry, Shadblow
Amelanchier

Sumac
Rhus

Viburnum
Viburnum

Wax Myrtle, Bayberry
Myrica, sometimes *Morella*

70 Beautyberry

Callicarpa

The list of birds that consume beautyberry fruits and seeds is a long one, including cardinals, mockingbirds, finches, woodpeckers, warblers such as the Black-throated Blue Warbler, and, especially, the Northern Bobwhite. Beautyberry is a host plant for caterpillars, so insectivorous birds appreciate it, too.

RECOMMENDED SPECIES

American beautyberry (*Callicarpa americana*) is the only species of *Callicarpa* native to North America, where it is restricted to southeastern states from Maryland to Missouri and Texas. Where it is locally native, it is easily propagated and requires little maintenance.

GRAY CATBIRD

NATIVE RANGE

USES
- Ornamental
- Hedgerow
- Land reclamation

EXPOSURE: Part shade

SOIL MOISTURE: Moist

MOST USEFUL SEASON(S): Year-round; may lose leaves in summer droughts

COLOR(S): Flowers white, pink; fruits purple

MAXIMUM HEIGHT: 6 feet (1.8 m)

71 Blackberry, Raspberry

Rubus

Even a fairly small raspberry or blackberry patch in your yard will welcome a big variety of birds. Raspberries host even more caterpillars than strawberries do, and their fruit is eaten by at least 150 different bird species. Their brambles provide nest cover for thrashers, cardinals, buntings, Yellow Warblers, and a lot of other birds as well.

YELLOW WARBLER

Raspberries, blackberries, and related fruits are not true shrubs but grow in impenetrable thickets called brambles and briars. Members of *Rubus* have been cultivated and hybridized for so long that their taxonomy is very jumbled. Loganberries, for example, are actually hybrids of

USES

- Hedgerow
- Reforestation
- Shade garden
- Ornamental
- Edible fruits

EXPOSURE: Shade to sun

SOIL MOISTURE: Dry to wet

MOST USEFUL SEASON(S): Spring to fall

COLOR(S): Flowers white, pink; fruits black, red

MAXIMUM HEIGHT: 12 feet (3.6 m)

NATIVE RANGE

raspberries and blackberries. Because of their popularity with gardeners and the fact that birds feeding on them propagate their seeds far and wide, the cultivars may be much more common even in natural habitat than the native species.

In forests where common blackberry grows, it's a very important pioneer plant in the understory. Its brambles protect tree seedlings until the growing saplings start shading the blackberry canes. Then the brambles die back until the next forest disruption.

If you don't want to share *all* of your berries, you can put bird netting over and around a section—but set it up so it's taut. Even then, you should monitor bird netting frequently in case a bird does get entangled.

RECOMMENDED SPECIES

Highbush or smooth blackberry (*Rubus canadensis*), native to much of the East, is listed as Endangered in New Jersey and Kentucky. Salmonberry (*R. spectabilis*), a West Coast native found naturally in cool forest stream banks, grows well in cool, shady gardens. Whitebark raspberry (*R. leucodermis*) is native in the West. The common blackberry (*R. allegheniensis*) is native in the East but is also established in the West.

72 Blueberry

Vaccinium

Plants in the genus *Vaccinium*, which includes huckleberries, lingonberries, cranberries, and other "heath" plants as well as blueberries, usually need acidic soils and cool temperatures. They host caterpillars that feed insectivorous birds, provide fruit for over 90 species of birds, and offer nest cover for such species as Chipping and Song Sparrows. Hummingbirds occasionally visit the flowers, especially of huckleberry, seeking nectar and small insects. Plants in this group are considered "prostrate shrubs"—true shrubs but very low to the ground.

Linnaeus first assigned the name *Vaccinium* to these plants from the classical Latin word for some of them. The name is not etymologically related to similar Latin words for cows or vaccinations.

YELLOW-FACED BUMBLE BEE

USES
- Hedgerow
- Edible fruits

EXPOSURE: Sun

SOIL MOISTURE: Dry to average

MOST USEFUL SEASON(S): Spring through fall

COLOR(S): Flowers white; fruits blue; fall leaves red

MAXIMUM HEIGHT: 8 feet (2.4 m)

NATIVE RANGE

RECOMMENDED SPECIES

The northern highbush blueberry (*Vaccinium corymbosum*), native to eastern Canada and New England west to Michigan and Wisconsin, is the species that has been hybridized and selectively bred for commercial blueberry production; it can be tricky to find plants that come from wild stock rather than cultivars. The lowbush blueberry (*V. angustifolium*) is the state fruit of Maine and the provincial berry of Nova Scotia. Lingonberry (*V. vitis-idaea*) is native throughout Canada, Alaska, and northern Minnesota through New England.

The fire-resistant thin-leaf huckleberry (*V. membranaceum*), one of the few plants that survived on the slopes of Mount Saint Helens when it erupted in 1980, is probably the same species of huckleberry that is considered the state fruit of Idaho. Mountain blueberry (*V. erythrocarpum*) is found in the Appalachians. Red huckleberry (*V. parvifolium*) is native and fairly common in forests from southeastern Alaska and British Columbia to central California.

Even the Deep South has some blueberries, such as Camp Darrow's blueberry (*V. darrowii*), native in the Gulf from Louisiana to Florida, and shiny blueberry (*V. myrsinites*), found in Florida, Alabama, Georgia, and South Carolina.

Top: Chipping Sparrows sometimes nest in *Vaccinium* shrubs. **Bottom:** Hermit Thrushes feed on blueberries wherever they can find them.

73 Buttonbush

Cephalanthus

In the East and South, buttonbush is one of the few native shrubs that provide midsummer blooms for pollinating insects and hummingbirds, and it hosts an excellent variety of larvae for insectivores. Waterfowl and other birds feed on the fruit and seeds. Found in swamps, floodplains, mangrove swamps, moist forests, and other wet habitats, it's one of the important natives in the Florida Everglades.

Wood Ducks prefer to nest in wetlands with a good understory of shrubs, buttonbush being one of the most effective at keeping swimming mammalian predators (like raccoons) from the nest tree. It's also the most common substory species where Prothonotary Warblers nest.

The town of Buttonwillow, California, is named for California buttonbush. On an old trans-San Joaquin Valley trail, a lone buttonbush served not only as an important landmark, but also as a meeting place for some of the Yokuts people.

RECOMMENDED SPECIES

Buttonbush (*Cephalanthus occidentalis*) has two natural varieties. Common buttonbush (*C. occidentalis* var. *occidentalis*) is found in eastern North America, ranging from Nova Scotia and Florida west to easternmost Minnesota and east Texas. California buttonbush (*C. occidentalis* var. *californicus*), the western form, has disjunct populations in California's entire San Joaquin Valley, mountain ranges in Arizona including the Mogollon Rim, and some areas of western Texas.

Two spectacular species, the Prothonotary Warbler (top) and Wood Duck (bottom), prefer nesting in cavities above an understory of buttonbush. This shrub offers protection from predators, insect food for the warbler, and fruits and seeds for the duck.

BUTTONBUSH

USES

- Hedgerow
- Reforestation
- Shade garden
- Wetland restoration
- Farm buffer/filter strip
- Ornamental

EXPOSURE: Part shade to shade, tolerating sun only where soils are wet

SOIL MOISTURE: Moist to wet

MOST USEFUL SEASON(S): Year-round

COLOR(S): Flowers white, pink

MAXIMUM HEIGHT: 12 feet (3.6 m)

NATIVE RANGE

74 Coralberry, Snowberry

Symphoricarpos

Nectar feeders, including hummingbirds, are strongly attracted to the tiny flowers of coralberry, some of the plants known as wolfberry, and the several species of snowberry. These plants all form fairly dense thickets, offering cover for nesting birds and forage areas for wintering birds. They also produce berries that feed a wide assortment of birds including robins, waxwings, grosbeaks, and mockingbirds.

RECOMMENDED SPECIES

Coralberry (*Symphoricarpos orbiculatus*) is an excellent choice in the eastern half of the continent, especially in shade or part shade and woodland gardens. Common snowberry (*S. albus*) and wolfberry (*S. occidentalis*) have very wide ranges. Individual wolfberry plants are short lived, but their suckers can ensure a long-standing thicket.

BLACK-CAPPED CHICKADEE

PINE GROSBEAK

NATIVE RANGE

USES

- Woodland garden
- Ornamental
- Erosion control
- Old-fashioned dooryard garden

EXPOSURE: Sun, part shade, shade

SOIL MOISTURE: Average

MOST USEFUL SEASON(S): Year-round

MAXIMUM HEIGHT: Flowers green, white, pinkish; berries pink, red, white

MAXIMUM HEIGHT: 12 feet (3.6 m)

CORALBERRY

SNOWBERRY

75 Crowberry

Empetrum

A "subshrub" that works well as a ground cover in shady, moist areas where the soil is acidic, crowberry provides fruits for more than 40 bird species, including Golden-crowned Sparrows and Snow Buntings. The berries often last through winter, revealed as snow melts to offer sustenance to early migrants.

Intriguingly, the black crowberry is native to the northern part of North America but not the central or southern states or anywhere in Central or South America except the Falkland Islands. Evolutionary biologists attribute that to seed dispersal by long-distance migrating birds.

SNOW BUNTING

RECOMMENDED SPECIES

Two crowberries are native to North America. Black crowberry (*Empetrum nigrum*) is found in the Cascades down to California, all the Canadian provinces, and the northernmost states from Minnesota and Michigan across to New England. Purple crowberry (*E. eamesii*) is found in the eastern half of that range, west only to Quebec in Canada and Minnesota in the United States.

CROWBERRY

USES
- Ground cover
- Ornamental

EXPOSURE: Sun, part shade, shade

SOIL MOISTURE: Dry, moist, wet

MOST USEFUL SEASON(S): Year-round

COLOR(S): Flowers pink, purple, red; fruits dark red to purple to black

MAXIMUM HEIGHT: 3 feet (1 m)

NATIVE RANGE

76 Desert-thorn, Wolfberry

Lycium

As the name indicates, desert-thorns are primarily found in arid and semi-arid areas in the Southwest. The berries are an important food for quail, Phainopeplas, and other birds; hummingbirds are attracted to the flowers for nectar. Desert-thorn also hosts insects that support insectivores.

Carolina wolfberry (*Lycium carolinianum*) grows in coastal areas, including places with rather high salinity. Ranging the farthest east of *Lycium* plants, Carolina wolfberry is found in the Gulf States and up the East Coast as far as Florida and South Carolina. Its berries ripen in October and November, just as Whooping Cranes arrive in Aransas National Wildlife Refuge in Texas after an arduous migration from Wood Buffalo National Park in Alberta. The cranes depend on Carolina wolfberry to replenish their energy and fat levels.

USES
- Ornamental
- Ground cover

EXPOSURE: Sun, part shade

SOIL MOISTURE: Dry or moist, depending on species

MOST USEFUL SEASON(S): Year-round

COLOR(S): Flowers lavender, blue, white; fruits red

MAXIMUM HEIGHT: 12 feet (3.6 m); most much smaller

NATIVE RANGE

RECOMMENDED SPECIES

A dozen or so species of desert-thorn are native to the Southwest. Some have very narrow habitat requirements; consult a native plant expert to identify the best choice(s) for your bird garden. The only native *Lycium* in the East, Carolina wolfberry, is mostly found in coastal areas of the Southeast.

No native *Lycium* species range into Canada or the northern states.

GAMBEL'S QUAIL

WHOOPING CRANES

77 Dogwood

Cornus

Whether growing as small trees, shrubs, or—in the case of bunchberry—a creeping ground cover, dogwoods are a rich source of berries that feed about 100 different bird species. Dogwoods also host a huge quantity of caterpillars, and most provide excellent cover for many nesting birds, including catbirds, thrashers, Bell's Vireo, and Summer Tanager.

BALTIMORE ORIOLE

SUMMER TANAGER

USES

- Ornamental
- Fencerows
- Ground cover
- Wildflower garden (bunchberry)

EXPOSURE: Shade, part shade, sun

SOIL MOISTURE: Moist

MOST USEFUL SEASON(S): Spring through fall

COLOR(S): Flowers white; fruits black, blue, red

MAXIMUM HEIGHT: 36 feet (11 m)

NATIVE RANGE

RECOMMENDED SPECIES

Check with experts on locally native plants to find out which dogwood(s) would be best for your situation—all of them are great choices as far as birds go. The flowering dogwood (*Cornus florida*—listed as Endangered in Ontario), round-leaf dogwood (*C. rugosa*), and pagoda dogwood (*C. alternifolia*) are three eastern species, the flowering dogwood ranging farther south than the other two.

Red osier dogwood (*C. sericea*) is a northern species ranging from the eastern provinces and New England across to parts of Alaska, British Columbia, and Washington and Oregon. Brown dogwood (*C. glabrata*) is limited to Oregon and California.

Bunchberry (*C. canadensis*) has a wide range and works well as a ground cover, especially where soils are acidic.

Cats and dogs may not always mix, but catbirds feast on dogwood berries.

78 Elderberry

Sambucus

At least 120 bird species eat the fruits of elderberries, which are particularly important for fueling the migration of Band-tailed Pigeons. Hummingbirds are attracted to the blossoms of some. Elderberry also hosts many species of insect larvae, providing food for an even wider assortment of birds. And to top it off, many birds, including warblers, grosbeaks, and goldfinches, nest in it.

RECOMMENDED SPECIES

The most widespread elderberries are red elderberry (*Sambucus racemosa*) and American black elderberry (*S. orbiculata*). In the West, blue elderberry (*S. cerulea*) and Rocky Mountain elderberry (*S. melanocarpa*) are important where they're locally native.

Unripe elderberry fruits can be toxic to humans.

Band-tailed Pigeon migration is fueled by fruits including elderberries.

NATIVE RANGE

USES
- Ornamental
- Edible fruits

EXPOSURE: Shade, part shade, sun

SOIL MOISTURE: Moist to wet

MOST USEFUL SEASON(S): Spring through fall

COLOR(S): Flowers white; berries red, black, blue

MAXIMUM HEIGHT: 20 feet (6 m)

79 Hawthorn

Crataegus

Often holding their fruits into winter, hawthorns provide essential food for thrushes, waxwings, and many other birds. The rest of the year, a great many birds visit hawthorns to feed on the many insects the plants host. Verdins, roadrunners, and Loggerhead Shrikes nest in the branches.

RECOMMENDED SPECIES

More than 200 species of hawthorns are native to North America. Although most occur east of the Rocky Mountains, some are locally native in the West. River hawthorn (*Crataegus rivularis*) is found in the temperate, intermontane regions of western mountains and is one of the two hawthorns that reach Arizona. Cerro hawthorn (*C. erythropoda*) has a more localized distribution in small areas of Arizona, New Mexico, and Colorado. Black hawthorn (*C. douglasii*) ranges from parts of the Canadian Atlantic coast to the West Coast as far north as southeastern

Alaska and south to California. The widespread fireberry hawthorn (*C. chrysocarpa*) is listed as Endangered in Indiana.

Hawthorns are indeed thorny. Some, such as cockspur hawthorn (*C. crus-galli*), have such low, densely set branches that it's difficult to maintain a lawn beneath them. Planting a shade-loving wildflower garden under the hawthorn can solve that problem.

English hawthorn (*C. monogyna*) is exotic in North America, and invasive.

AMERICAN ROBIN

VERDIN

HAWTHORN

USES
- Ornamental

EXPOSURE: Sun, part shade, shade

SOIL MOISTURE: Average to moist

MOST USEFUL SEASON(S): Year-round

COLOR(S): Flowers white, pink; fruits red, purple, black, yellow

MAXIMUM HEIGHT: 36 feet (11 m)

NATIVE RANGE

Hazelnut

Corylus

 ALLERGEN

Hosting at least 124 different insect larvae, this shrub provides food for a great many insectivores. Its nuts are eaten by turkeys, woodpeckers, jays, and other birds; the catkins are a staple for Ruffed Grouse in winter. Unfortunately, hazel pollen is often the cause of allergies in late winter and early spring.

RECOMMENDED SPECIES

American hazelnut (*Corylus americana*) is native to the eastern half of the continent west to Manitoba down to Missouri. Beaked hazelnut (*C. cornuta*) has a more limited range in the East but has a disjunct western variety, the California hazelnut (*C. cornuta* var. *californica*).

NATIVE RANGE

USES
- Ornamental
- Hedgerow/thicket
- Edible nuts

EXPOSURE: Sun, part shade, shade

SOIL MOISTURE: Average to moist

MOST USEFUL SEASON(S): Year-round

COLOR(S): Flowers white, green; catkins yellowish brown; fall foliage bright yellow to deep wine-red

MAXIMUM HEIGHT: 12 feet (3.6 m)

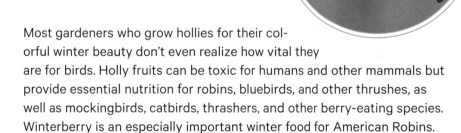
PYRRHULOXIA

81 Holly

Ilex

⚠
NONNATIVE
SPECIES
INVASIVE

Most gardeners who grow hollies for their colorful winter beauty don't even realize how vital they are for birds. Holly fruits can be toxic for humans and other mammals but provide essential nutrition for robins, bluebirds, and other thrushes, as well as mockingbirds, catbirds, thrashers, and other berry-eating species. Winterberry is an especially important winter food for American Robins.

When holly berries first turn red, they may taste too bitter even for birds. With repeated freezing and thawing, however, they become sweet, which means they are still around and most palatable just when other winter fruits have been depleted.

Don't bother growing a single holly tree or shrub. Hollies have separate male and female plants, and a male plant must be nearby for insects, especially bees, to pick up the pollen to pollinate nearby female plants. Three female shrubs in the vicinity of one male can provide a good balance for fruit production.

continued on next page

NATIVE RANGE

USES
- Hedgerow
- Reforestation
- Shade garden

EXPOSURE: Part shade

SOIL MOISTURE: Moist to wet

MOST USEFUL SEASON(S): Year-round

COLOR(S): Flowers white; fruits red

MAXIMUM HEIGHT: 9 feet (2.7 m)

RECOMMENDED SPECIES

Native hollies are eastern species. The American holly (*Ilex opaca*), the state tree of Delaware, retains its brilliant, beautifully shaped leaves through winter, contrasting perfectly with the bright red berries. Winterberry (*I. verticillata*), another native holly that is extremely important for birds, does lose its leaves, but the brilliance of the berries makes up for it. Possumhaw (*I. decidua*), Carolina holly (*I. ambigua*), and inkberry (*I. glabra*) are other good choices in the Southeast.

English holly (*I. aquifolium*) has become an invasive pest crowding out native species where it's been planted in the West—especially in the Pacific Northwest—and should be removed.

WINTERBERRY

82 Honeysuckle

Lonicera

**NONNATIVES
INVASIVE**

Honeysuckle is one of those miracle plants that provides for a host of birds in a host of ways. A great many bird species, from quail to Purple Finches, eat the fruits; hummingbirds and orioles come to the nectar. Many caterpillars feed on the leaves, and scores of tiny flying insects feed on the flowers and berries, providing food for a wide assortment of insectivores. And many birds such as catbirds, cardinals, mockingbirds, and Song Sparrows nest in the thick branches. Some native honeysuckles produce nectar-rich flowers from spring through summer.

So what's the problem?

Several exotic honeysuckles have been introduced in North America, and Japanese honeysuckle (*Lonicera japonica*) in particular is terribly invasive, crowding out native shrubs. Nesting birds suffer significantly more nest failures in Japanese honeysuckle than in native species. Never

continued on next page

NATIVE RANGE

USES
- Ornamental
- Hedgerow
- Fencerows

EXPOSURE: Sun, part shade

SOIL MOISTURE: Average

MOST USEFUL SEASON(S): Spring through fall

COLOR(S): Flowers white, red, purple, orange; fruits red

MAXIMUM HEIGHT: 10 feet (3 m)

plant any honeysuckles that are not locally native. And if you have Japanese honeysuckle on your property, do your best to root it out.

RECOMMENDED SPECIES

Any locally native *Lonicera* will be welcomed by your local birds. Some, such as western white honeysuckle (*L. albiflora*), Arizona honeysuckle (*L. arizonica*), and orange honeysuckle (*L. ciliosa*) can grow as vines, climbing walls and columns. The blossoms of orange honeysuckle attract many humming-birds in the West, as do the long red blossoms of trumpet honeysuckle (*L. sempervirens*), which ranges in the East.

RUBY-THROATED
HUMMINGBIRD

PURPLE FINCH

83

Leadplant

Amorpha

   **INVASIVE WHERE NOT LOCALLY NATIVE**

Like other legumes, leadplant enriches the soil as it grows. It's found primarily in drier soils in its range and often appears in the same habitats as the prairie grass little bluestem (*Schizachyrium scoparium*).

It can take five years for a leadplant to reach maturity and finally start flowering, but even when young it hosts a significant variety of caterpillars, and nectar-feeding insects add to the insectivore diet when it finally starts blooming.

Leadplant is shorter than the similar false indigo (*Amorpha fruticosa*), another North American native, and found in drier habitats.

continued on next page

Tufted Titmice are among the birds that feed on leadplant seeds.

RECOMMENDED SPECIES

Leadplant (*Amorpha canescens*) is slow growing and not prolific enough to be considered weedy anywhere in its range. It grows well in dry, poor soils so makes a good choice when reclaiming old strip-mines, gravel pits, and similar badly treated sites.

False indigo (*A. fruticosa*) is rare in West Virginia, Manitoba, and Ontario, but it is considered a noxious weed in 46 states and is banned in Connecticut and Washington. Bird gardeners should pay close attention to which *Amorpha* they're planting.

LEADPLANT

NATIVE RANGE

USES

- Hedgerow
- Prairie restoration/ wildflower meadow
- Reclaimed industrial land/ tough sites
- Pasture/rangeland
- Farm buffer/filter strip
- Ornamental

EXPOSURE: Sun

SOIL MOISTURE: Dry to wet

MOST USEFUL SEASON(S): Summer

COLOR(S): Flowers purple

MAXIMUM HEIGHT: 10 feet (3 m)

84 Manzanita, Bearberry

Arctostaphylos

Related to blueberries, manzanitas are extraordinarily rich in nectar—some people say the nectar can even be shaken from flowers on warm days. Hummingbirds are naturally drawn to that.

This large family has its greatest diversity in the West, particularly California. Bearberry (*Arctostaphylos uva-ursi*), which also grows in the East, is named for the way bears are drawn to its berries—if they can get to them before birds and small mammals eat them.

Manzanitas provide food for avian insectivores by hosting many caterpillars, including some that develop into showy and rare butterflies and moths. And the dense foliage provides excellent nest cover.

continued on next page

RECOMMENDED SPECIES

Most manzanitas are western species. Any locally native ones are fine choices.

Bearberry has the widest distribution of North American manzanitas, extending throughout the western third of the continent and through central and eastern Canada and the northern states. It has been extirpated in Ohio and Pennsylvania, however, and is listed as Endangered in Illinois and Iowa and Rare in Indiana.

Wrentits often nest in shrubby, low-growing manzanita.

MANZANITA, BEARBERRY

NATIVE RANGE

USES

- Hedgerow
- Reforestation
- Ornamental
- Rock garden

EXPOSURE: Sun

SOIL MOISTURE: Average

MOST USEFUL SEASON(S): Spring through fall

COLOR(S): Flowers white, pink

MAXIMUM HEIGHT: 20 feet (6 m)

85 Rhododendron, Azalea

Rhododendron

Native species of the genus *Rhododendron*, which encompasses both rhododendrons and azaleas, include some of the most beautiful plants we can grow in a bird garden. Hummingbirds drink the nectar, grouse feed on the buds, and Rose-breasted Grosbeaks and Swainson's Warblers nest within rhododendron thickets.

SWAINSON'S WARBLER

ROSE-BREASTED GROSBEAK

continued on next page

NATIVE RANGE

USES

- Hedgerow
- Reforestation
- Shade garden
- Ornamental

EXPOSURE: Sun to shade

SOIL MOISTURE: Average to moist

MOST USEFUL SEASON(S): Spring through fall

COLOR(S): Many

MAXIMUM HEIGHT: 20 feet (6 m)

RECOMMENDED SPECIES

Rhododendron is the state flower of West Virginia. In the East, smooth azalea (*Rhododendron arborescens*), piedmont rhododendron (*R. minus*), and early azalea (*R. prinophyllum*) are all readily available from nurseries. In the West, look for western azalea (*R. occidentale*), Pacific rhododendron (*R. macrophyllum*), and the Cascade azalea (*R. albiflorum*).

Flame azalea (*R. calendulaceum*) has been extirpated from Pennsylvania and is listed as Endangered in Ohio, and swamp azalea (*R. viscosum*) is listed as Endangered in Maine, Threatened in New Hampshire, and Exploitably Vulnerable in New York.

CARDINAL CHICKS

FLAME AZALEA

86

Rose

Rosa

    SOME SPECIES INVASIVE

As beautiful as roses are to us, they're probably even more beautiful to birds. Our native roses provide abundant insects for insectivores. The fruits, called rose hips, often last into winter, providing sustenance for at least 42 bird species.

For many birds such as towhees, native sparrows, Indigo Buntings, and cardinals, even the thorns on rosebushes are desirable features, protecting them from predators.

RECOMMENDED SPECIES

More than 20 species of roses are native in North America. Woods' rose (*Rosa woodsii*) and Nootka rose (*R. nutkana*) are common and easy to grow. Smooth rose (*R. blanda*) is the state flower of Kansas and North Dakota; it's listed as Endangered in Maryland and Threatened in Ohio. In the Midwest and East, some of the widely distributed choices are Virginia rose (*R. virginiana*), Carolina rose (*R. carolina*), swamp rose (*R. palustris*), and climbing rose (*R. setigera*).

continued on next page

CEDAR WAXWING

Tragically, some of the wild roses people are most familiar with, including beach rose (*R. rugosa*), multiflora rose (*R. multiflora*), and, ironically, the state flower of Georgia, the Cherokee rose (*R. laevigata*), are from other continents and have become invasive here. Native species provide every advantage that the exotic wild roses do, without the problems.

Eastern Towhees are among the many birds that feed on rose hips; they also nest in roses.

ROSE

NATIVE RANGE

USES
- Hedgerow
- Wildflower meadow/ prairie restoration
- Farm buffer/filter strip
- Ornamental
- Edible fruits

EXPOSURE: Sun to part shade

SOIL MOISTURE: Wet to dry

MOST USEFUL SEASON(S): Year-round until buried in snow

COLOR(S): Flowers white, yellow, red, pink; fruits red

MAXIMUM HEIGHT: 12 feet (3.6 m)

87 Sagebrush
Artemisia

Primarily found in the American West, *Artemisia* includes sagebrush and wormwood. Sagebrush is a critical component of essential habitat for Greater and Gunnison Sage-Grouse and many other habitat specialists.

Much more widespread than sagebrush, Louisiana sage is found throughout the continent except in Alaska and Florida. Western populations of Louisiana sage tend to grow in lowlands; eastern populations, in uplands.

Sagebrush Sparrows are named for one of the plants they require to survive.

continued on next page

219

NATIVE RANGE

USES
- Ornamental
- Ground cover

EXPOSURE: Sun

SOIL MOISTURE: Dry

MOST USEFUL SEASON(S): Year-round

COLOR(S): Foliage blue-gray; flowers yellow

MAXIMUM HEIGHT: 12 feet (3.6 m)

RECOMMENDED SPECIES

Big sagebrush (*Artemisia tridentata*), the most typical of Western sagebrush, is an attractive, gnarled shrub. Other sagebrush and wormwoods can have fairly localized ranges; locally native species are worth considering.

Louisiana sage (*A. ludoviciana*) can be grown as a ground cover; it even allows mowing.

YELLOW-HEADED BLACKBIRD

GREATER SAGE-GROUSE

Close Connection

Greater and Gunnison Sage-Grouse really live up to their name. Sagebrush is an essential component of their diet year-round, and they select sagebrush almost exclusively for cover. Male sage-grouse plumage is extremely conspicuous when males are displaying, but during their day-to-day life when not displaying, their plumage, as in the females, is cryptically colored to blend in with sagebrush.

88

Saw Palmetto

Serenoa

Found nowhere else, saw palmetto is an essential component of ecosystems in subtropical Florida and along the Gulf Coast to east Texas. The Florida Scrub-Jay, listed as Threatened, and the Burrowing Owl, listed as State Threatened in Florida, frequent scrubby habitats where saw palmetto is an important component.

More than 100 bird species—and gopher tortoises as well as many other animals—feed on the fruits. Many birds also feed on the insects drawn to saw palmettos, and the plants provide essential cover for many species for nesting and during the heat of midday.

continued on next page

GOPHER TORTOISE

221

PALM WARBLER

Close Connections

Florida Scrub-Jays almost never wander beyond the edges of scrub habitat, and development has left them with isolated islands of habitat rather than large, connected swaths. Floridians who are committed to planting scrub oaks, saw palmettos, and other native plants in their own yards and in public spaces are performing a vital service for these splendid birds.

FLORIDA SCRUB-JAY

Saw palmetto is extremely long lived, some plants enduring for hundreds of years and quickly resprouting after fires. Fire suppression, development, and the planting of invasive exotics have reduced its habitat to a tiny fraction of what it historically was.

RECOMMENDED SPECIES

Saw palmetto (*Serenoa repens*), the only species in this genus, is endemic to the subtropical southeastern United States. It can be difficult to grow from seed; nurseries often have small plants that are easier to establish.

SAW PALMETTO

NATIVE RANGE

USES
- Reforestation
- Shade garden
- Wetland restoration

EXPOSURE: Part shade

SOIL MOISTURE: Well drained or seasonally waterlogged

MOST USEFUL SEASON(S): Year-round

COLOR(S): Flowers white

MAXIMUM HEIGHT: 10 feet (3 m)

EASTERN BLUEBIRD

89 Serviceberry, Juneberry, Shadblow

Amelanchier

Birds crowd to serviceberry for the rich assortment of insects these small trees and shrubs host and, of course, for the berries. Also called juneberry and shadblow, these plants are some of the earliest flowering and fruiting shrubs and small trees. Spectacular swallowtail butterflies are among the huge variety of caterpillars serviceberries host.

Unfortunately, rabbits and deer browse heavily on serviceberry in winter unless the shrubs are well protected.

continued on next page

Cedar Waxwings (left) and Red-bellied Woodpeckers (right) are among the many birds that devour serviceberries.

RECOMMENDED SPECIES

Common serviceberry (*Amelanchier arborea*) is an ideal bird-attracting tree or shrub over much of the East, barely north into Canada, and absent in the Gulf and southern Atlantic coasts; it's not found in Florida. The oblong-fruit serviceberry (*A. bartramiana*) ranges farther north into Canada, but not as far south as *A. arborea*.

Some *Amelanchier* may have different cultivars that grow as trees or as shrubs. Make sure the plant you get is suited for your needs as well as locally native.

SERVICEBERRY, JUNEBERRY, SHADBLOW

NATIVE RANGE

USES
- Ornamental
- Edible fruits

EXPOSURE: Sun, part shade, shade

SOIL MOISTURE: Average

MOST USEFUL SEASON(S): Early spring into summer

COLOR(S): Flowers white; fruits red, blue-purple

MAXIMUM HEIGHT: 36 feet (11 m)

90

Sumac

Rhus

**POISON SUMAC
HIGHLY TOXIC**

In all seasons, sumac is an essential plant for birds. Catbirds, thrashers, and other birds feed on the fruits and hide within the foliage for nesting and cover. Aphids and other insects feed on the plants in summer, luring hummingbirds and other insectivores.

In areas where fruiting shrubs and trees are abundant, sumac fruits may be ignored by some species at first, but they become vital food for birds in late winter and early spring when other fruits have been depleted. Early-arriving robins,

STAGHORN SUMAC

continued on next page

NATIVE RANGE

USES

- Ornamental
- Hedgerow
- Fencerows
- Erosion control
- Land reclamation
- Edible fruits

EXPOSURE: Sun, part shade, shade

SOIL MOISTURE: Dry to moist

MOST USEFUL SEASON(S): Year-round

COLOR(S): Fruit red, deep purple, brownish; fall foliage red; flowers yellow, green, white, brown

MAXIMUM HEIGHT: 25 feet (7.6 m)

flickers, and other birds feast on the fruits during late snowstorms.

Poison sumac (*Toxicodendron vernix*) was once included in *Rhus* but has a complicated taxonomy. It produces the same skin-irritating oil, urushiol, as poison ivy and poison oak, and scientists currently place them all in the same genus. Poison sumac grows in wet and clay soils in the eastern half of the continent, where it is easily mistaken for smooth sumac. Birds love it, but it is even more toxic to people than poison ivy and poison oak.

RECOMMENDED SPECIES

Virtually all sumacs attract birds. Most thrive in clumps, and many spread via suckers so don't work well in small gardens. Smooth sumac (*Rhus glabra*) is the only shrub or tree native to all 48 contiguous states (and much of Canada as well). Staghorn sumac (*R. typhina*), limited to the East, is very

NORTHERN CARDINAL

STAGHORN SUMAC

popular for its fall foliage. It grows in dry, poor soil where many other plants can't thrive.

California's lemonade sumac (*R. integrifolia*), an evergreen shrub found naturally on ocean bluffs, in canyons, and in dry places below 2,500 feet (760 m), is often used for erosion control. Greater Roadrunners are fond of its berries. Little-leaf sumac (*R. microphylla*), of western Texas, southwestern New Mexico, and southeastern Arizona, is a very important wildlife plant in its dry range.

GREATER ROADRUNNER

GRAY CATBIRD

91 Viburnum

Viburnum

About 100 different species of larvae feast on North America's viburnums, attracting a rich assortment of insectivores. Hummingbirds visit the flowers and many birds feast on the berries.

RECOMMENDED SPECIES

Southern arrowwood viburnum (*Viburnum dentatum*), found in much of the southeastern quarter of the continent, and its northern counterpart (*V. recognitum*) are the most soil-adaptable of the viburnums. If you're purchasing arrowwood viburnum, make sure you purchase the right species—avoid *V. carlesii*, which is not native but has been naturalized in Ohio.

Despite its name, the common viburnum (*V. ellipticum*) is native only from Washington to central California, in forests and mountain chaparral habitat. Nannyberry (*V. lentago*) is widespread in the northern

USES
- Ornamental

EXPOSURE: Sun, part shade, shade

SOIL MOISTURE: Moist

MOST USEFUL SEASON(S): Year-round

COLOR(S): Flowers white; berries red, purple, black; fall foliage may be bronze-red

MAXIMUM HEIGHT: 36 feet (11 m)

NATIVE RANGE

two-thirds of the continent east of the Rocky Mountains. Many birds feed on nannyberries in winter.

The American cranberrybush (*V. trilobum*) is not a cranberry but is often called highbush cranberry. It's closely related to the European viburnum (*V. opulus*), and the North American species is sometimes called *V. opulus* var. *americanum*.

Blackhaw (*V. prunifolium*) is listed as Threatened in Connecticut.

No viburnums are native in the desert Southwest, where many nurseries sell species from other continents. To support native wildlife, it's much wiser to choose locally native plants that provide some of the same gardening values.

AMERICAN ROBIN

CEDAR WAXWING

WILLOW MINING BEE

92 Wax Myrtle, Bayberry

Myrica, sometimes *Morella*

TREE SWALLOW

Extremely popular with birds because of their nutritious berries, wax myrtles and bayberries are important sources of food in winter. They also host many insect larvae.

A great variety of birds eat the berries. Yellow-rumped Warblers have the northernmost winter range of eastern warblers, specifically because they can digest the waxy coating of these berries. The Yellow-rumped Warbler's eastern sub-species, the Myrtle Warbler, is even named for its close association with wax myrtle. Most warblers are almost exclusively insectivores.

Tree Swallows survive cold spells by feeding on the berries when flying insects aren't available.

These plants have nitrogen-fixing nodules on their roots, allowing them to grow on poor soils.

RECOMMENDED SPECIES

It can be tricky to purchase locally native wax myrtles and bayberries, in part because some taxonomists place some of them in *Morella*. Two are most consistently called *Myrica*. Sweetgale (*Myrica gale*) ranges from coast to coast in Canada and Alaska as well as in Washington and Oregon and the northeastern states east of Minnesota. It's an excellent choice for lakeside property on northern, boggy lakes; White-throated and Swamp Sparrows nest in it. The Sierra bayberry (*M. hartwegii*) is endemic to the Sierra Nevada in California, where it's found in moist areas in the foothills and lower slopes.

The other species of wax myrtle and bayberry are often placed in *Morella*. The northern bayberry (*M. pensylvanica*) is listed as Endangered in Ohio and as Exploitably Vulnerable in New York; southern bayberry (*M. cerifera*) is listed as Endangered in Maryland. The Pacific wax myrtle or California bayberry (*M. californica*) is found in coastal areas from Vancouver Island in British Columbia through Washington, Oregon, and California. It is very tolerant of beach wind.

One subspecies of Yellow-rumped Warblers is also called the Myrtle Warbler for its dependence on wax myrtle fruit in winter.

WAX MYRTLE, BAYBERRY

USES
- Ornamental
- Screening
- Hedgerow

EXPOSURE: Sun, part shade

SOIL MOISTURE: Moist to wet

MOST USEFUL SEASON(S): Year-round

COLOR(S): Berries white, pale blue

MAXIMUM HEIGHT: 36 feet (11 m)

NATIVE RANGE

VINES

Backyard landscapers often use vines to cover old fences, trellises, unattractive poles, and the sides of buildings. Those tangles of vines can also provide hideouts and shelter for many birds.

Vines selected specifically for bird gardens also provide an abundance of nectar and fruits while harboring nutritious insects to feed a wide variety of birds.

Clematis
Clematis

Trumpet Vine
Campsis

Virginia Creeper, Woodbine
Parthenocissus

Wild Grape
Vitis

SCARLET LEATHER FLOWER

VIRGIN'S BOWER

93 Clematis

Clematis

**NONNATIVES
VERY INVASIVE**

A lovely flowering vine often grown on fences or trellises, clematis sometimes attracts hummingbirds as well as butterflies with its nectar. It also hosts caterpillars that feed many other birds, produces seeds that many birds eat, and provides secluded nesting spots for songbirds.

ROBIN'S NEST

ANNA'S
HUMMINGBIRD

continued on next page

233

NATIVE RANGE

USES
- Ornamental
- Trellises

EXPOSURE: Sun, part shade

SOIL MOISTURE: Dry to wet, depending on species

MOST USEFUL SEASON(S): Early summer through early fall

COLOR(S): Flowers white, red, purple, blue, yellow, pink

MAXIMUM HEIGHT: Climbing, 20 feet (6 m)

RECOMMENDED SPECIES

Most clematis originated in China and Japan, and some of those species are invasive here. In particular, *Clematis terniflora*, a Japanese species often sold in nurseries and garden centers, can quickly become invasive. But several clematis species are native to North America.

Swamp leather flower (*C. crispa*), also called blue jasmine, is listed as Endangered in Illinois and Threatened in Kentucky. Vasevine (*C. viorna*) is Endangered in Illinois and Pennsylvania. Scarlet leather flower (*C. texensis*) is pretty enough to be planted in gardens in many areas but is endemic only to the Edwards Plateau in Texas.

In the West, the hairy clematis (*C. hirsutissima*), also called lion's beard, grows as a small perennial rather than a vine. Western white clematis (*C. ligusticifolia*) is very attractive to butterflies and birds, including hummingbirds.

SWAMP LEATHER FLOWER

HAIRY CLEMATIS

94

Trumpet Vine

Campsis

    ⚠ ROOTS AGGRESSIVE

Virtually guaranteed to attract Ruby-throated Hummingbirds, the woody trumpet vine is the primary host of trumpet vine sphinx moths. When allowed to grow densely, the foliage offers an attractive nesting site for some songbirds. The plant's aerial rootlets work their way into wood, stone, and brick, so don't plant it near your house or on a fragile trellis.

RECOMMENDED SPECIES

Trumpet vine (*Campsis radicans*) is our only native *Campsis*. It's thick growing and can become locally invasive, especially in the Southeast. Many people plant it in an area of their property where they can mow to keep it from spreading.

RUBY-THROATED HUMMINGBIRD

USES
- Ornamental
- Fencerows
- Erosion control

EXPOSURE: Sun

SOIL MOISTURE: Dry to moist

MOST USEFUL SEASON(S): Late spring to fall

COLOR(S): Flowers red, orange, yellow

MAXIMUM HEIGHT: 72 feet (22 m) with support structures

NATIVE RANGE

95 Virginia Creeper, Woodbine

Parthenocissus

**NONNATIVES
INVASIVE**

The fruits of Virginia creeper and its relatives are valuable for birds (although most are toxic to humans) and can remain on the vines well into winter, providing food for many overwintering birds as well as autumn migrants. These plants are rich in caterpillars, including several sphinx moths, and many birds roost and nest within the dense foliage, including House Finches, Bushtits, Gray Catbirds, and Brown Thrashers.

RECOMMENDED SPECIES

Virginia creeper (*Parthenocissus quinquefolia*) adheres to structures via adhesive discs rather than rootlets that damage buildings, so it is sometimes planted on sun-exposed walls of brick buildings. The thicket creeper (*P. inserta* or *vitacea*), with a range that extends farther west, climbs via twirling tendrils rather than adhesive discs and cannot climb up smooth

USES
- Ornamental
- Fencerows
- Trellises and walls

EXPOSURE: Shade, part shade, sun

SOIL MOISTURE: Dry, medium, moist

MOST USEFUL SEASON(S): Year-round

COLOR(S): Foliage red in fall; fruit black, blue; flowers greenish, inconspicuous

MAXIMUM HEIGHT: Can climb to 40 feet (12 m)

NATIVE RANGE

SPHINX MOTH CATERPILLAR

ROSE-BREASTED GROSBEAK

walls. The seven-leaf creeper (*P. hep-taphylla*), endemic to the Edwards Plateau and the Lampasas Cut Plain of Central Texas, lacks adhesive discs on the tendrils and so is less likely to climb walls.

Despite its name and its storied presence on the brick outfield walls at Wrigley Field in Chicago, Boston ivy (*P. tricuspidata*) is neither an ivy nor native to Boston or anywhere else in North America.

Boston ivy is often grown to cover the facades of masonry buildings, shading the walls, lowering cooling costs, and reducing dependence on air conditioning during summer, but Virginia and thicket creepers perform just as well, so there isn't a real benefit to using a nonnative plant for this purpose.

96
Wild Grape
Vitis

Humans aren't the only fans of grapes—more than 100 bird species have been recorded feasting on the fruits. When orioles in the East overwinter north of their normal winter range, they often do so where fruit still clings to wild grapevines. Insectivores are drawn to grapes, too, for the many caterpillars the plants host and the flying insects attracted by the sweet fruit. And grape tangles are perfect for concealing songbird nests.

RECOMMENDED SPECIES
More than a dozen wild grape species are native to North America, and many areas have a few locally native choices. Planting two or three different species can provide fruit during a wider window of time than choosing just one.

Baltimore Orioles feed heavily on grapes, and during the period when they overwinter in northern states, wild grapes are often nearby.

USES

- Ornamental
- Ground cover
- Fencerows
- Trellises
- Erosion control
- Edible fruits

EXPOSURE: Sun, part shade, shade

SOIL MOISTURE: Moist to dry

MOST USEFUL SEASON(S): Spring, summer, fall, winter until fruit is gone

COLOR(S): Flowers white, yellow, green; fruits blue, purple

MAXIMUM HEIGHT: Many to 30 feet (9 m), a few to 100 feet (30 m) on trees and other structures

NATIVE RANGE

Some of our native grapes are in trouble and would benefit from fostering. Sand grape (*Vitis rupestris*) is listed as Endangered in Indiana and Pennsylvania, Threatened in Kentucky, and of Special Concern in Tennessee. Summer grape (*V. aestivalis*) is listed as Endangered in Maine.

V. vinifera, native around the Mediterranean and in central Asia, is the grape most important for commercial production, but several native North American grapes are also cultivated, so even people growing grapes for human consumption and wine production may have locally native choices.

NORTHERN CARDINAL

HOUSE SPARROW

CACTUS AND YUCCA

Succulents, such as cacti and yuccas, are specially adapted for dry habitats, but the natural ranges of a few species extend as far north as Canada.

Of course, most cacti are native only to deserts. There, conscientious landscaping for birds means growing native plants that can thrive with natural rainfall levels, requiring no additional watering.

Cholla and Prickly Pear
Cylindropuntia, Opuntia

Hedgehog Cactus
Echinocereus

Ocotillo
Fouquieria

Yucca, Joshua Tree
Yucca

CHOLLA

PRICKLY PEAR

97 Cholla and Prickly Pear

Cylindropuntia, Opuntia

⚠ **SPINES HIGHLY TOXIC**

Combined in the genus *Opuntia* until recently, cholla and prickly pear are both important for birds. Desert birds flock to them to eat fruits and seeds. Cactus Wrens, Curve-billed Thrashers, and Black-throated Sparrows often sing from cholla tops and nest in these plants, along with Mourning and Inca Doves, Greater Roadrunners, and Lucifer Hummingbirds.

CURVE-BILLED THRASHER

LUCIFER HUMMINGBIRD

continued on next page

NATIVE RANGE CHOLLA

NATIVE RANGE PRICKLY PEAR

USES
- Borders
- Ground cover
- Xeriscaping
- Ornamental
- Edible fruits (prickly pear)

EXPOSURE: Sun

SOIL MOISTURE: Dry

MOST USEFUL SEASON(S): Year-round

COLORS: Flowers red, pink, purple, green, yellow, orange

MAXIMUM HEIGHT: 15 feet (4.5 m)

The barbed, hairlike spines of these cacti can be brutal to handle. The tiny spines, called glochids, can cause extreme skin irritation when touched.

RECOMMENDED SPECIES

About 20 species of cholla are native to the southwestern states east to Texas and Oklahoma. One hardy species that ranges from the hot deserts of west Texas to the Colorado mountains above 6,000 feet (1829 m) is the tree cholla (*Cylindropuntia imbricata*). Some range across several states while others have much narrower ranges, so talk to a native plant expert in your area to select the right ones for your property.

Prickly pears are far more widespread; more than three dozen species are native to the United States, three of them reaching Canada: brittle prickly pear (*Opuntia fragilis*), eastern prickly pear (*O. humifusa*), and

BROAD-TAILED HUMMINGBIRD

Cactus Wrens (upper right) and Mourning Doves (lower right) are among the birds that nest in cholla and prickly pears.

plains prickly pear (*O. polyacantha*). Eastern prickly pear is listed as Endangered in Massachusetts, of Special Concern in Connecticut, Exploitably Vulnerable in New York, and Rare in Pennsylvania.

Although some species are very widespread, others are much more localized, so make sure to check with a native plant expert to choose the right one for your locality. Select a species that's the right size for your garden—many are very low growing, but some can be the size of small trees.

98

Hedgehog Cactus

Echinocereus

Easier to cultivate than many other cacti, hedgehog cactus is an excellent choice for beginning gardeners in the Southwest trying their hand at xeriscaping. Wherever red-flowered cacti are in bloom, hummingbirds zip in, and Broad-tailed Hummingbirds are especially attracted to red-flowered hedgehog cactus.

RECOMMENDED SPECIES

The dozens of species native in the United States each have specific requirements, so any locally native species sold by knowledgeable nurseries can be excellent choices. These cacti are fairly small. They shouldn't be crowded, but even the smallest desert yard can accommodate a few.

BROAD-TAILED HUMMINGBIRD

NATIVE RANGE

USES
- Ornamental
- Xeriscaping

EXPOSURE: Sun, part shade

SOIL MOISTURE: Dry

MOST USEFUL SEASON(S): Year-round

COLOR(S): Flowers red, purple

MAXIMUM HEIGHT: 3 feet (1 m)

99

Ocotillo

Fouquieria

Although it appears cactuslike, ocotillo is actually related to blueberries. For most of the year it resembles a bundle of dead, spiny sticks, but lush leaves emerge in the monsoon season and it blooms after rainfall. The bright crimson flowers draw many birds for nectar, the insects attracted to the flowers, and the seeds.

Lucifer Hummingbirds, Verdins, and Curve-billed Thrashers nest in ocotillo. Costa's Hummingbird arrives when ocotillo is blooming, nesting close so females can feed near the nest.

RECOMMENDED SPECIES

Ocotillo (*Fouquieria splendens*) is the only ocotillo that ranges north of Mexico.

SCOTT'S ORIOLE

USES
- Ornamental
- Xeriscaping

EXPOSURE: Part shade

SOIL MOISTURE: Dry

MOST USEFUL SEASON(S): Year-round

COLOR(S): Flowers red, orange

MAXIMUM HEIGHT: 36 feet (11 m)

NATIVE RANGE

100

Yucca, Joshua Tree

Yucca

New Mexico's state flower, yucca is an important plant of dry habitats because most species provide a host of caterpillars for insectivores. Hummingbirds and orioles are drawn to the nectar-rich flowers of some yuccas (others are pollinated by nocturnal moths) and a variety of birds are attracted to yucca fruits. Verdin, Mourning Dove, and House Finch nest in them.

Yucca leaves can be stiff, serrated along the edges, and sharp-pointed—plants named for daggers and bayonets got those names for a reason! So be careful not to plant yuccas near sidewalks or other pathways where people pass close by.

Yuccas make stunning additions to desert yards, especially when in bloom. The Joshua tree (*Yucca brevifolia*), iconic in the Mojave Desert, adds a dramatic touch for landscapers where it's native in California, Nevada, Utah, and Arizona.

USES
- Ornamental
- Xeriscaping

EXPOSURE: Sun

SOIL MOISTURE: Dry

MOST USEFUL SEASON(S): Year-round

COLOR(S): Flowers white

MAXIMUM HEIGHT: 40 feet (12 m)

NATIVE RANGE

RECOMMENDED SPECIES

The genus *Yucca* is widespread, but most species have fairly small ranges. In the Southeast, Spanish dagger (*Y. aloifolia*) tolerates salt spray and ranges naturally along the coasts from east Texas to North Carolina. Spanish bayonet or moundlily yucca (*Y. gloriosa*) is much more limited to sand dunes on the Atlantic coast and barrier islands from southern Virginia to northern Florida. Contact with the leaves can cause skin irritation.

Adam's needle (*Y. filamentosa*), found naturally as far north as southeast Virginia, has been introduced beyond its range along the Eastern Seaboard as far as Long Island Sound, and even into the Midwest. When planting for birds north of Virginia, it's wiser to choose locally native plants. A yucca moth is important for pollinating Adam's needle, but hummingbirds also come to the flowers.

Another plant called Spanish bayonet (*Y. harrimaniae*) is found in the Southwest in Nevada, Utah, Arizona, and Colorado. Texas yucca (*Y. rupicola*) is restricted to Texas.

Top: A Ladder-backed Woodpecker samples Joshua tree flowers.
Bottom: An Anna's Hummingbird visits a yucca.

FAVORITE PLANTS
of Common North American Birds

Most birds are "generalists," not associated with single species of plants, and even "specialists" nest and feed in a variety of plants associated with their particular habitat. But some birds do best when particular plant species are available, and a few absolutely require a particular plant for food, nesting, or both.

SPECIES	PREFERRED FOOD(S)	NESTING CHOICES
Gray Catbird	Dogwood and other native berries	Often nests in dogwood and sumac
Whooping Crane	Carolina wolfberry when first arriving at the Gulf after fall migration	Nests on the tundra
Cassia Crossbill	Rocky Mountain lodgepole pine seeds	Rocky Mountain lodgepole pine
Red Crossbill	Pine seeds	Pines
Black-billed Cuckoo	Forest tent caterpillars in aspen forests	Usually in deciduous trees near caterpillar outbreaks
Wood Duck	Acorns	Prefers nest-cavity tree where buttonbush grows underneath
Bald Eagle	Fish	Old white pines, often a mile or more from the nearest fishing area
American Goldfinch	Native thistle and milkweed seeds	Uses the down from thistles and milkweed as nesting material
Evening Grosbeak	Boxelder and maple seeds, spruce budworm	Nests in a variety of trees
Ruffed Grouse	Aspen catkins	Generally nests in stands of young trees
Spruce Grouse	Spruce needles in winter	Spruce
Anna's Hummingbird	Fuchsia-flowered gooseberry, native sages	Nests in a variety of plants and human-built constructions
Broad-tailed Hummingbird	Especially attracted to red-flowered hedgehog cactus	Nests in a variety of plants
Costa's Hummingbird	Feeds heavily in ocotillo	Nests near ocotillo
Ruby-throated Hummingbird	Cardinal flower, beebalm, jewelweed, red columbine, trumpet vine	Lichens (and spider silk) as nest materials
Rufous Hummingbird	Fireweed, native sages, golden-beard penstemon	Nests in a variety of plants
Blue Jay	Acorns as primary food	Nests in a variety of trees
Pinyon Jay	Pinyon pine cones	Conifers near productive pinyon pines
White-breasted Nuthatch	Feeds in a variety of trees	Often nests in maple

SPECIES	PREFERRED FOOD(S)	NESTING CHOICES
Baltimore Oriole	Berries, fruits, and nectar from a variety of trees, especially redbud in early spring	American elm, basswood
Northern Parula	Native trees providing insects	Spanish moss or *Usnea* lichen, depending on range
Band-tailed Pigeon	Elderberry fruits to fuel migration	Nests in a variety of plants
Common Redpoll	Tamarack and birch seeds; alder, aspen, birch catkins	Tundra
Greater and Gunnison Sage-Grouse	Sagebrush leaves	On the ground beneath sagebrush
Sapsuckers	Often drills holes for insects in aspen, alder, birch, and mountain ash	Trees infested with heart rot
Florida Scrub-Jay	Acorns from scrub oak	Prefers nesting in live oak
Brown Thrasher	Dogwood and other native berries	Often nests in dogwood and sumac
Bicknell's Thrush	Browses on fruits and small arthropods near or on the ground, usually near stunted balsam firs	Balsam fir
Wood Thrush	Small prey in leaf litter, especially in beech-maple areas	Incorporates dead beech leaves into nests
Verdin	Feeds in a variety of plants	Often nests near desert willow, desert hackberry, ocotillo, and Joshua tree
Black-capped Vireo	Insects from various scrub vegetation	Low, scrubby vegetation, especially scrub oak
Hermit Warbler	Insects high in the branches of old-growth Douglas fir	Often nests high in old-growth Douglas fir
Kirtland's Warbler	Insects associated with jack pine stands	Nests only under jack pine trees
Swainson's Warbler	Various insects	Often nests in rhododendron
Yellow-rumped Warbler	Wax myrtle berries in fall and winter	Nests in a variety of northern forests
Bohemian Waxwing	Mountain ash berries	Nests in a variety of trees
Cedar Waxwing	Cedar/juniper "berries" (tiny bluish cones); cherry and apple blossoms in spring	Many trees including cedar/juniper
Acorn Woodpecker	Acorns; often build granaries in sycamore	Nests in a variety of trees
Ladder-backed Woodpecker	Feeds in a variety of trees	Very often nests in desert willow
Pileated Woodpecker	Insects in rotting or infested wood	Often nests in aspens infected with heart rot
Red-cockaded Woodpecker	Insects under the bark of pine trees	Longleaf pine
White-headed Woodpecker	Ponderosa pine	Ponderosa and other large pines

North American Native Plant Societies

NATIVE PLANT SOCIETIES IN THE UNITED STATES

Alabama	Alabama Wildflower Society	www.alwildflowers.org
Alaska	Alaska Native Plant Society	https://aknps.org
Arizona	The Arizona Native Plant Society	https://aznps.com
Arkansas	Arkansas Native Plant Society	https://anps.org
California	California Native Plant Society	https://cnps.org
Colorado	Colorado Native Plant Society	https://conps.org
Connecticut	Connecticut Botanical Society (see also New England)	https://ct-botanical-society.org
Delaware	Delaware Native Plant Society	https://delawarenativeplants.org
Florida	Florida Native Plant Society	https://fnps.org
Georgia	Georgia Native Plant Society	https://gnps.org
Hawaii	Native Hawaiian Plant Society	www.hear.org/nhps
Idaho	Idaho Native Plant Society	https://idahonativeplants.org
Illinois	Illinois Native Plant Society	https://illinoisplants.org
Indiana	Indiana Native Plant Society	https://indiananativeplants.org
Iowa	Iowa Native Plant Society	www.iowanativeplants.org
Kansas	Kansas Native Plant Society	https://kansasnativeplantsociety.org
Kentucky	Kentucky Native Plant Society	https://knps.org
Louisiana	Louisiana Native Plant Society	https://lnps.org
Maine	See New England	
Maryland	Maryland Native Plant Society	https://mdflora.org
Massachusetts	Grow Native Massachusetts (see also New England)	https://grownativemass.org
Michigan	The Michigan Botanical Club	www.michbotclub.org
Minnesota	Minnesota Native Plant Society	https://mnnps.org
Mississippi	Mississippi Native Plant Society	https://mississippinativeplantsociety.org
Missouri	Missouri Native Plant Society	https://monativeplants.org
Montana	Montana Native Plant Society	https://mtnativeplants.org
Nebraska	Nebraska Native Plant Society	https://nebraskanativeplantsociety.weebly.com
Nevada	Nevada Native Plant Society	https://nvnps.org
New England	Native Plant Trust New England Botanical Club	www.nativeplanttrust.org https://rhodora.org
New Hampshire	See New England	
New Jersey	The Native Plant Society of New Jersey	https://npsnj.org
New Mexico	Native Plant Society of New Mexico	https://npsnm.org

New York	New York Flora Association	https://nyflora.org
North Carolina	North Carolina Native Plant Society	https://ncwildflower.org
North Dakota	Great Plains Native Plant Society	https://gpnps.org
Ohio	Midwest Native Plant Society	https://midwestnativeplants.org
Oklahoma	Oklahoma Native Plant Society	https://oknativeplants.org
Oregon	Native Plant Society of Oregon	https://npsoregon.org
Pennsylvania	Pennsylvania Native Plant Society	https://panativeplantsociety.org
Rhode Island	Rhode Island Wild Plant Society (see also New England)	https://riwps.org
South Carolina	South Carolina Native Plant Society	https://scnps.org
South Dakota	Great Plains Native Plant Society	https://gpnps.org
Tennessee	Tennessee Native Plant Society	https://tnps.org
Texas	Native Plant Society of Texas	https://npsot.org/wp
Utah	Utah Native Plant Society	https://unps.org
Vermont	Vermont Botanical & Bird Club (see also New England)	https://vtbb.org
Virginia	Virginia Native Plant Society	https://vnps.org
Washington	Washington Native Plant Society	https://wnps.org
West Virginia	West Virginia Native Plant Society	www.wvnps.org
Wisconsin	Botanical Club of Wisconsin	https://sites.google.com/site/botanicalclubofwisconsin
Wyoming	Wyoming Native Plant Society	www.wynps.org

NATIVE PLANT SOCIETIES IN CANADA

Alberta	Alberta Native Plant Council	https://anpc.ab.ca
British Columbia	Native Plant Society of British Columbia	https://npsbc.wordpress.com
Manitoba	Native Orchid Conservation Inc.	https://nativeorchid.org/wordpress
New Brunswick	The New Brunswick Botany Club	https://nbbotanyclub.wordpress.com
Newfoundland and Labrador	The Wildflower Society of Newfoundland and Labrador	https://wildflowersocietynl.ca
Nova Scotia	Nova Scotia Wild Flora Society	www.nswildflora.ca
Ontario	North American Native Plant Society	https://nanps.org
Quebec	FloraQuebeca	https://floraquebeca.qc.ca
Saskatchewan	Native Plant Society of Saskatchewan	https://npss.sk.ca

Index

Entries in **bold** type indicate plant profiles. Entries highlighted in color indicate where terms are defined.

Interior Photography Credits

© 49pauly/iStock.com, 226; © abrunk/iStock.com, 152 b.l.; © AGAMI Photo Agency/Alamy Stock Photo, 43 b.; © Agami Photo Agency/Shutterstock.com, 104 l.; © agefotostock/Alamy Stock Photo, 230 t.l.; © Akchamczuk/iStock.com, 146 l.; © Aksana Kavaleuskaya/stock.adobe.com, 35; © Ald Ro/Alamy Stock Photo, 79 b.; © Alina Boldina/Shutterstock.com, 14; © Alina Vaska/Shutterstock.com, 60 m.; © All Canada Photos/Alamy Stock Photo, 38 m., 57 b.r., 173 b.l.; © ALong/Shutterstock.com, 177 t.; © AlpamayoPhoto/iStock.com, 4 r.; © Andrew Sabai/Shutterstock.com, 135 l.; © AnkNet/iStock.com, 208; © Anna Lurye/stock.adobe.com, 188 l.; © argenlant/123RF.com, 57 t.r.; © ArtBoyMB/iStock.com, 227 t.r.; © Aubrey Huggins/Alamy Stock Photo, 207 t.; © Avalon.red/Alamy Stock Photo, 233 t.l.; © b2bjacks/stock.adobe.com, 129, 159 b.; © benfosterphotography/iStock.com, 94 t.; © Beth Baisch/stock.adobe.com, 222 r.; © bgwalker/iStock.com, 60 t.; © Bildagentur-o/stock.adobe.com, 134 r.; © Bildagentur Zoonar GmbH/Shutterstock.com, 111 main; © Bill Gorum/Alamy Stock Photo, 101 t.r.; © BIOSPHOTO/Alamy Stock Photo, 141 t.; © BirdImages/iStock.com, 87 b., 233 b.l.; © blickwinkel/Alamy Stock Photo, 68 t., 95 t.r., 141 b.r., 167 l., 176 b., 179 b.; © Bobbushphoto/iStock.com, 85 b.; © Bob Gibbons/Alamy Stock Photo, 173 t., 247 t.; © bob.stock.adobe.com, 12 b.c.; © bookguy/iStock.com, 34 t.; © Brett/stock.adobe.com, 59 l.; © Brian A Wolf/Shutterstock.com, 58 t.; © BrianLasenby/iStock.com, 92 t.; © Brian Lasenby/Shutterstock.com, 132 b.; © cantelow/123RF.com, 57 t.l.; © Casey E Martin/stock.adobe.com, 133 t.; © Cavan/stock.adobe.com, 6–7; © Cavan Images/Alamy Stock Photo, 137; © Cecile Marion/Alamy Stock Photo, 69 b.; © Charles/stock.adobe.com, 73 r.; © Charles Bergman/Shutterstock.com, 217 b.; © Charles Melton/Alamy Stock Photo, 244 b.; © Charles T. Peden/Shutterstock.com, 19; © Christina Rollo/Alamy Stock Photo, 63; © Christopher/stock.adobe.com, 228 r.; © ChuckSchugPhotography/iStock.com, 154 t.; © Claudia Wizner/stock.adobe.com, 116 m.; © ClubhouseArts/iStock.com, 80 t.; © coco/stock.adobe.com, 5 l.; © Crowing Hen/Shutterstock.com, 101 b.r.; © cturtletrax/iStock.com, 106 l., 221 t.r., 230 t.r.; © cweimer4/iStock.com, 70 l.; © daniel/stock.adobe.com, 237 r.; © Daniel Dempster Photography/Alamy Stock Photo, 179 t.l.; © Danita Delimont/Alamy Stock Photo, 62 b., 99 l., 163, 183 b., 229 t., 239 r., 243 b.; © Danita Delimont Creative/Alamy Stock Photo, 124 r.; © Danita Delimont/Shutterstock.com, 201; © Danita Delimont/stock.adobe.com, 152 t.; © danlogan/iStock.com, 61 r.; © Daria Katiukha/Shutterstock.com, 160 b.; © DaveAlan/iStock.com, 56 t.; © David/stock.adobe.com, 8 r.; © DavidByronKeener/iStock.com, 148; © davidgater74/stock.adobe.com, 155 t.; © David McGowen/stock.adobe.com, 34 b.; © Daybreak Imagery/Alamy Stock Photo, 224 r.; © Daybreak Imagery/Animals Animals/agefotostock, 233 b.r.; © Dee Browning/Shutterstock.com, 90 t.; © Denise Erickson/iStock.com, 24; © denisveselyxx/stock.adobe.com, 159 t.; © Diane Labombarbe/iStock.com, 23 t.; © DK Photography/stock.adobe.com, 204 l.; © Don/stock.adobe.com, 220 t.; © Don Johnston/All Canada Photos Inc./agefotostock, 9 t.c.; © Don Johnston_ON/Alamy Stock Photo, 64 t.; © Dopeyden/iStock.com, 44 t.; © Doug McCutcheon/Alamy Stock Photo, 50 r.; © driftlessstudio/iStock.com, 238 t.; © dszc/iStock.com, 93 t.l.; © Dylan Brew/Shutterstock.com, 51; © EdwinWilke/Shutterstock.com, 95 b.; © Elenathewise/stock.adobe.com, 142 t.; © Elle777/Shutterstock.com, 158 b.; © Emanuel Tanjala/Alamy Stock Photo, 233 t.r.; © emer1940/iStock.com, 203 t.; © Erik/stock.adobe.com, 9 b.l., 139 t.; © fgsmiles/stock.adobe.com, 138 t.; © FloralImages/Alamy Stock Photo, 18; © Florapix/Alamy Stock Photo, 204 r.; © Florist Kuniko/Shutterstock.com, 81 t.; © FLPA/Alamy Stock Photo, 128 b.l.; © flycatdesign/stock.adobe.com, 12 t.l.; © FotoRequest/stock.adobe.com, 22 l.; © Funtay/iStock.com, 87 t.; © gardenlife/Shutterstock.com, 134 l.; © gardenlife/stock.adobe.com, 169 l.; © Gay Bumgarner/Alamy Stock Photo, 123; © George E. Stewart/Dembinsky Photo Associates/Alamy Stock Photo, 127 l.; © Ger Bosma/Alamy Stock Photo, 72 m.; © Gerald Corsi/iStock.com, 78 l., 101 l., 198 r.; © Gerry/stock.adobe.com, 131, 187; © Gerry Bishop/Alamy Stock Photo, 172 b., 174 r.; © Gerry Bishop/Shutterstock.com, 146 r.; © Gfed/iStock.com, 32; © gjohnston-photo/iStock.com, 15 r.; © GordonImages/iStock.com, 4 l., 37 t.; © gpflman/iStock.com, 110 b.; © Gratysanna/iStock.com, 4 c.; © Grigorii_Pisotckii/iStock.com, 196 t.; © Grigoriy/stock.adobe.com, 121 t.; © GummyBone/iStock.com, 230 b.; © gurineb/iStock.com, 156 m.; © Hal Beral/VWPics/Alamy Stock Photo, 166 b.; © HealerTeresa/iStock.com, 94 b.; © Hector Cordero/Alamy Stock Photo, 26; © Holcy/iStock.com, 42 r.; © hstiver/iStock.com, 210 b.; © iDiscoverer/Shutterstock.com, 213 l.; © ilonal/stock.adobe.com, 119 l.; © Imladris01/iStock.com, 174 l.; © IrinaK/Shutterstock.com, 165 r.; © islavicek/Shutterstock.com, 74 t.; © Iva Vagnerova/iStock.com, 195 b.; © Jack/stock.adobe.com, 200 m.; © JackVandenHeuvel/iStock.com, 52 r.; © James Cheak Photography/Alamy Stock Photo, 234 l.; © james metcalf/EyeEm/stock.adobe.com, 243 t.r.; © Jan/stock.adobe.com, 25; © Jared Quentin/stock.adobe.com, 5 r.; © Jason Ondreicka/Alamy Stock Photo, 237 l.; © JasonOndreicka/iStock.com, 44 b.; © Jaynes Gallery/Danita Delimont/iStock.com, 73 l.; © JeannetteKatzir/iStock.com, 66 b.r.; © jeanro/iStock.com, 9 t.r.; © Jeff Huth/iStock.com, 16 l., 136 b.l.; © Jim and Lynne Weber/Shutterstock.com, 241 b.l., 247 b.; © Joan Budai/Shutterstock.com, 41b.; © joemeyer/stock.adobe.com, 239 l.; © Johann Schumacher/Alamy Stock Photo, 142 b.; © John Cancalosi/agefotostock/agefotostock, 75; © John Martin/Alamy Stock Photo, 96 l.; © John Richmond/Alamy Stock Photo, 151; © John Wright/stock.adobe.com, 245 t.; © JP/stock.adobe.com, 76 r.; © Judy Freilicher/Alamy Stock Photo, 71 b.; © Julian Popov/Shutterstock.com, 212; © jwjarrett/stock.adobe.com, 227 b.r.; © JZHunt/iStock.com, 71 t., 161 r.; © Karel Bock/iStock.com, 156 b.; © Kathleen Gail/iStock.com, 171; © Kativ/iStock.com, 38 t.; © kburgess/stock.adobe.com, 147 m.; © Keith/stock.adobe.com, 136 l.; © Kelly Haller/stock.adobe.com, 9 t.l.; © Kelly/stock.adobe.com, 149 l.; © kellyvandellen/iStock.com, 216 r.; © Kerry Hargrove/stock.adobe.com, 219 t.r.; © Kevin Schafer/Alamy Stock Photo, 190 b.; © kivitimof/iStock.com, 181 t.; © kmm7553/stock.adobe.com, 23 b.; © kristina rütten/stock.adobe.com, 168; © kristyewing/iStock.com, 66 t.; © Krumpelman Photography/Shutterstock.com, 96 r.; © K Steve Cope/Shutterstock.com, 43 t.r.; © Lakeview_Images/iStock.com, 107 t., 145 b.; © Lari Bat/iStock.com, 116 t.; © Lasse Hendriks/stock.adobe.com, 54 b.r.; © Laura Erickson, 3, 20, 37 b., 42 l., 49 l., 52 t.l. & b.l., 55 b., 57 b.l., 60 b., 65, 66 b.l., 69 t.l., 80 b., 83 t., 84, 85 t., 98 t., 100, 104 t.r. & b.r., 107 b., 109 l., 110 t., 113 b., 115, 117, 120, 121 b., 127 r., 128 b.r., 133 m., 136 b.r., 138 b., 140, 143, 145 t.r., 147 b., 150,

continued on next page